Student Transitions from Middle to High School

Improving Achievement and Creating a Safer Environment

J. Allen Queen

EYE ON EDUCATION
6 DEPOT WAY WEST
LARCHMONT, NY 10538
(914) 833-0551
(914) 833-0761 fax
www.eyeoneducation.com

Library of Congress Cataloging-in-Publication Data

Queen, J. Allen.
    Student transitions from middle to high school: improving achievement
and creating a safer environment / J. Allen Queen.
    p. cm.
    Includes bibliographical references (p.).
    ISBN 1–930556–37–3
    1. Articulation (Education)—United States. 2. Middle school education—
United States. 3. Education, Secondary—United States. 4. Student
adjustment–United States. I. Title.

LB1626.Q44 2002
373.12'1—dc21

2002020507

10 9 8 7 6 5 4 3 2

Editorial and production services provided by
City Desktop Productions, LLC
10127 Northwestern Avenue, Franksville, WI 53126
(262-884-8822)

Also available from Eye On Education

TEACHING IN THE BLOCK:
STRATEGIES FOR ENGAGING ACTIVE LEARNERS
Edited by Canady and Rettig

THE 4 x 4 BLOCK SCHEDULE
Queen and Isenhour

TEACHER RETENTION: WHAT IS YOUR
WEAKEST LINK?
India Podsen

HANDBOOK ON TEACHER PORTFOLIOS FOR
EVALUATION AND PROFESSIONAL DEVELOPMENT
(includes CD-ROM)
Tucker, Strong, and Gareis

COACHING AND MENTORING FIRST-YEAR AND
STUDENT TEACHERS
Podsen and Denmark

DIFFERENTIATED INSTRUCTION:
A Guide for Middle and High School Teachers
Amy Benjamin

MOTIVATING AND INSPIRING TEACHERS:
THE EDUCATOR'S GUIDE FOR BUILDING
STAFF MORALE
Whitaker, Whitaker, and Lumpa

DEALING WITH DIFFICULT TEACHERS
Todd Whitaker

ASSESSMENT IN THE BLOCK: THE LINK
TO INSTRUCTION
McCullough and Tanner

SUPERVISION AND STAFF DEVELOPMENT
IN THE BLOCK
Zepeda and Mayers

Live in the now;
With all of its problems and its agonies;
With its joy and its pain.
Celebrate your pain,
Your despair,
Your anger,
It means you're alive.
Look deeper
Breathe deeper.
Stand taller.
Stop grieving the past.
There is joy and beauty today.

—Anonymus

*To my son, Alex, who survived and succeeded
in ninth grade.*

Acknowledgements

Most of this book comes from the contributions of many practicing educators working daily with students in various phases of transition. As superintendents, principals and teachers, many in dual roles as graduate students, discovered the impact transitions have on student achievement and safety, and these same individuals in assisting with this book have perhaps saved thousands of students from the perils of failure to be included in the growing epidemic of becoming a "high school dropout." I am sure that I have unintentionally left out some names of individuals who were instrumental in making this book a reality. To those individuals, I extend my appreciation and ask for their pardon. It is with special thanks that I acknowledge their direct and indirect contributions to this book. These include the following superintendents and principals: Donna Cianfrani, Martin Eaddy, Jeannie Freshcorn, Randi Imbriano, Rick Hinson, Darrin Hartness, Richard Lancaster, Debra Morris, Barrett Mosbacker, Janice Ritter, Abdenabi Senbel, Victoria Walker, Jim Watson, Betty Wecker, and James Williams. Also, because teachers believe that every child has a right to be successful and safe in school, I would like to thank the following: James Burnham, Kristy Bullock, Jenny Burrell, Acquanetta S. Edmond, Vance Fishback , Patricia Gibson, Tonya Kales, Chris Lineberry, Ashlee Luff, Bryan Lynip, Wendy Gravely, Damon Rhodes, Jodi L. Weatherman, and Sheryl Wilson.

About the Author

Dr. J. Allen Queen serves as Professor and Chair in the Department of Educational Leadership in the College of Education at The University of North Carolina at Charlotte. He has served as a major consultant in block scheduling, classroom management, and safe schools to school systems throughout the United States.

He has been a classroom teacher, principal, curriculum specialist, professor and college administrator. Dr. Queen has presented at international, national and state conferences and he has authored numerous books and professional journals in the field of education.

Dr. Queen resides in Kings Mountain, North Carolina with his wife, Patsy and his tenth-grade son, Alex.

Table of Contents

Queen's Twelve Factors for Successful Transitions

The author has studied the idea of transitions for several years. As a ninth-grade teacher, I remember the students' fear, some masked by excitement, of the ninth-grade experience. I often wondered if it was just normal stress that goes with any change. I am convinced that much of the success individuals have in their lives can be contributed to how successful they were in the act of "transitioning." To a greater degree, I have discovered what I believe to be the common factors that we as educators have ignored for years to be signals or warning signs that we must be able to identify and correct. Therefore, I have done three things to provide evidence to my claims. First, I have included the twelve factors that are based upon collaborated research within the preface. Please read these closely. Second, within the book, I have tried to embed the related factors on transitions from the research into practice, and finally in Appendix A, I have restated my twelve factors, identified the related research, and provided an analysis on some of the larger studies.

Factor One
The lower the students' grades drop during ninth-grade transition, the higher the students' probability of dropping out of school.

Factor Two
Students who fail during the transition and drop out of school experience lifelong difficulties physically, socially, emotionally and economically.

Factor Three
The larger the high school, the greater the negative impact of transition on ninth grade students.

Factor Four
Students, once in school, who experience two or more transitions prior to ninth-grade have a greater probability of quitting high school.

Factor Five
High school dropout rates are higher for middle school students than for students attending K-8 schools.

Factor Six
Ninth-grade students' adjustments to high school are complicated by their perceptions of a bigger school, different environment, changed class schedule and smaller classes.

Factor Seven
Fear of getting lost in the high school building is by far the number one fear of ninth-grade students.

Factor Eight
Ninth-grade students view high school teachers less helpful than middle school teachers.

Factor Nine
Ninth-grade students must have at least one adult in their lives for genuine support in order to become academically and socially successful.

Factor Ten
Ninth-grade students who have negative experiences during the transitional period have poor attendance, low grades and fewer friends. They tend to become behavior problems and have greater vulnerability to negative peer influence.

Factor Eleven
Dropout rates increase for poorly transitioned, especially minority students, in schools using high-stakes testing.

Factor Twelve
Social and economic factors negatively impact graduation rates, especially in large urban areas.

1

From Middle School to High School

Most students attending public school today will experience several formal transitions, or the process of moving from one level of schooling to another, prior to kindergarten and concluding after graduating from high school. Five major transitions from home to college can be identified for most students.

We usually think of the first transition as from home to kindergarten, but for a growing segment of the population there is a variety of formal experiences such as church preschool, Head Start or private day-care that actually serve as the first transition from home to a group setting. Few parents keep their children at home exclusively before kindergarten. In the second transition, most children attend an elementary school that ranges from kindergarten through the fifth grade. Students are exposed to the third formal transition with the middle school experience beginning in sixth grade and culminating in eighth grade, or in some instances, ninth grade. Thereafter, students transition into high school for the fourth experience, usually ranging from grade nine or ten through twelve. Upon the completion of the twelfth grade, students have their fifth transition by entering college/post secondary education or the workforce. Not surprising is the fact that some students have more transitions than these four if their family moves often or they attend schools having unusual organizational patterns. It is the fourth transition, or the move from middle school to high school, that will be the focus of this book.

The transition from middle school to senior high school can be traumatic for young adolescents, yet it is considered to be another rite of passage in life that young people must experience in order to move to the next level of education.

This chapter continues by identifying strategies that can ease the transition from the middle school to the senior high school. Throughout the chapter, the areas emphasized are the perception of students and parents with respect to transition, a review of the methods for easing the transition, and the related duties and responsibilities of the school administrator, the teacher, and the school guidance counselor.

It is important to understand that in implementing any type of transition program there must be substantial support, a level of preparedness and continued consistency throughout the process. In order for this implementation to be successful, individual needs and group needs must be considered.

Two Different Types of Transitions

There are two distinct forms of transition. One form of transition is systematic and built into the structure of the public school system; the other is developmental and incorporates physical, intellectual, social and emotional change. From this perspective, systematic transitions include the process that occurs during the changes in the various levels found within the educational system, and the second form references the various types and stages of development from early childhood to early adulthood.

The main function of the first stage of transition is usually for basic childcare or to compensate for limited or inefficient developmental experiences, but many social skills, both positive and negative, may be experienced for the first time. During the second transition to the elementary school beginning at kindergarten, the focus shifts to a greater emphasis on basic skills in literacy and mathematics, and in most classrooms, an intentional attempt to teach the process of socialization. As the student moves to the third transition, from elementary to middle school, we see a greater emphasis on the mastery of basic skills, more content in social studies and the sciences, and in the better classrooms, teachers challenging students with higher levels of problem solving and character development. From middle school to high school, which emphasizes a balanced curriculum focusing on the acquisition of knowledge and developing a conceptual understanding across various subjects, students experience the fourth and often most challenging transition that will occur: The ninth grade and starting high school.

Varying concerns surface during the transition of students from one school level to the next, ranging from issues involving various teaching methods to the actual learning process. Researchers studying school transitions believe that the transitions between schools need to be smooth to avoid extremely drastic changes and to limit the negative impact on students. In the age of high-stakes testing and an underestimated number of students quitting school, many transitionalists advocate that it is imperative that well developed programs be implemented to maximize student success (Balfanz and Legters 2001). We will review this process in much greater detail later in the book.

The General Impact of Student Transitions

Students affected by the transition from middle school to high school are often classified by gender, behavior problems, low academic performance, or socio-economic status. At one time females had the most difficulty with the transition to high school, but with the age of terrorism and school violence, the anxiety has balanced equally to males and females. Peer relations are extremely important to both male and female students. Upon entering the high school, students of both genders often find it extremely difficult to adjust because their friendship circle has been disconnected.

Another problem that is evident during the transition process involves those who experienced behavioral difficulties during the elementary school years. Students with behavioral problems constantly disrupt the class setting and often end up in confrontations with other students or the classroom teacher. These students have an extremely difficult time adjusting to any school environment and most will become serious discipline problems in middle school and high school (Queen 2002).

Students sometimes experience difficulty making a successful transition because they are not academically prepared for the next school level. Due to an inadequate preparation for the next level, they often make lower scores on tests, fail to complete homework assignments, and rarely comprehend the assigned activity. This leads to higher levels of frustration, failure, and once at high school, the greater probability of dropping out of school.

Sadly, most individuals affected by the transition periods are students from low socio-economic environments. Many African American and Hispanic students living in poverty may lack the parental support that could enable them to make more successful transitions. These support structures include the degree of parental interest and participation in school and related events, and the extent to which parents supplement the learning process with educational activities. Perhaps the most important factor is the degree parents have conversations with their children about school and learning.

African American males are identified as the individuals who experience the most difficulty when making a successful transition from the middle school to the high school. In many cases, African American males fall into categories pertaining to behavior problems, low academic performance, and low socio-economic status. The problem may be the result of a disproportionate representation of African American males that are in classes designed for learning-disabled students, which usually results in an inappropriate placement because of classroom behavior. Once a student is placed outside the realm of the education process, the placement begins to take a form and procedure that inhibits learning opportunities, which in turn become fewer opportunities, which negatively impacts the school experience (Anderson, Jacobs, Schramm, and Splittgerber 2000; Hauser, Simmons, and Pager 2001).

School boards and administrators have struggled with the question of which organizational pattern best serves the needs of students. For economic and educational reasons the most common configurations include grades K-5, 6-8, and 9-12; grades K-6, 7-9, and 10-12; grades K-6 and 7-12; and grades K-12 in single-school districts (Freshcorn 2000). In all but one configuration, students face at least two and often three school transitions as they progress through the public school organization. A related issue is the recent proliferation of the middle school, grades 6-8. With such a config-uration, many students must adapt to a school transition between the fifth and sixth grades and the eighth and ninth grades. This has become more of a problem that may have been overlooked with all the excitement and promise of the middle school movement.

The Schools and Transitions

Public schools were formed during the colonial period. Stu-dents were housed in the same building under the instruction of one teacher. Students were taught basic academic and social skills in order to participate in a largely rural economy. However, this organizational structure was insufficient to meet the growing socio-economic needs of American society. With increased indus-trialization and urbanization, societal needs precipitated the development of the high school. During the last quarter of the nineteenth century, public high schools spread rapidly through-out the United States.

The elementary and high school structures remained intact until the introduction of the junior high school (grades 7-9) in the 1920's. Critics of the junior high school argued that it resembled high school too closely, ignoring the unique needs of adolescents during a unique developmental stage in their lives. The middle school movement (encompassing grades 6-8), developed from this criti-cism. The purpose of the middle school remains today to serve as a transition for students as they develop from childhood into ado-lescence. The middle school incorporates programs and structures uniquely designed for students at this developmental stage. The middle school movement gained strength throughout the country and expanded rapidly during the 1980's (McEwin 1990).

The popularity of the middle school concept, coupled with eco-nomic and demographic indicators, has caused an increased num-ber of students to face school transition between the eighth and ninth grades. The National School Board Association (1997) predicts that student enrollment will peak in this country by the year 2007, with the highest increase at the high school level. Financially, school boards are spending substantial funds to improve existing facilities. If the middle school is to remain as an accepted school structure, we must be aware of student problems following a school transition between the eighth and ninth grade.

Several theories attempt to explain adolescent development. Most textbooks include three main areas of cognitive, social, and physical development. A challenge to those of us working with middle school and high school students is to gain a better understanding of adolescent behavior. Detailed information on the stages of human growth and development is an essential starting point of the process and can be found in numerous education and psychology textbooks.

The critical transition from middle school to high school occurs as students are experiencing the pain of adolescence. This significant move into a new school involves "disrupting relationships with teachers and peers at a time when teenagers are becoming more independent from their families and experiencing less parental involvement in their schooling" (Schiller 1999). "During the first year of high school, students encounter a new social environment in which they are unknown to teachers and many peers and at a stage when their identity is formative. High school represents both an opportunity to develop in new or continuing directions and also the risk of being perceived in terms limited to ethnicity or academic competence" (Oxley, Croninger, and DeGroot 2000). While some students are successful in using this opportunity to redefine themselves socially or academically, the competitive and impersonal environment of the high school devastates others. "The larger size of high schools and the tendency of secondary school teachers to use less individualized instruction and to base assessment of student progress on social comparisons increase the latter risk" (Oxley et al. 2000). The success or failure experienced during this transition can be the turning point in the social and academic lives of students (Schiller 1999).

Understanding adolescence and the needs of the students is crucial, not only in providing the necessary support for these students, but also for building a program that reflects the needs of all students. According to the work done by Zsiray, Larsen, and Liechty (1996), teenagers generally need the following: to develop their own values and not just parrot their parent's ideas; to find out what they can do and be proud of their own accomplishments;

to develop close relationships with boys and girls their own age; and to be accepted, loved, and respected for who they are and what they believe. The most important task of the adolescent is the search for identity. The search occurs in three primary ways: by developing values, by developing pride in one's achievements, and by developing close relationships with peers. By secondary school age, "students have gained the cognitive ability to reflect on themselves and often experience self-consciousness, and they have begun to interact with wider, more diverse groups that are removed from family and neighborhood. These are the conditions that permit adolescents to explore and experiment with different roles and interests and later to achieve more sustained commitments and identifications" (Oxley et al. 2000). The challenge then becomes, how do educators build a school program that allows students to search for their identity and be successful academically and socially?

As middle school students move to high school, they encounter the opportunity to make new friends and have more choices. Conversely, they have an increased opportunity to be picked on and teased by older students, to get lost, to receive harder work, and to make lower grades. These student problems can be limited by providing a supportive middle school environment with a transition program addressing the needs of students and their parents that facilitates communication between middle school and high school educators (Mizelle 1999).

It is important to remember that early adolescence is a stage of thinking for students. At this point in life, adolescents think and develop 'what if' situations as they begin to experience both the joys and challenges of this new stage. Cognitive development encompasses ways in which one perceives, interprets, and reacts to the environment. These interactions allow the adolescent to develop strategies to learn to make positive decisions and resolve personal conflict (Queen 1999).

The change in thinking abilities impacts the early adolescent's outlook on life in general, and affects social interaction. In terms of socialization, the adolescent is extremely interested in socializing or interacting with his or her peers, and they have a strong need to fit into the group.

Because the feeling of belonging is such a high priority to many adolescents, submitting to peer pressure is common, and the early adolescent follows fads and often worries about measuring up to idealized standards that have been established by peers, often from unreliable to even ridiculous sources. Peer relationships tend to be an important source of support for adolescents, and developing relationships is a very important goal (Hicks 1997). Additionally, these individuals have become more self-conscious and usually overly concerned about other people's reaction to them. They become increasingly concerned with their appearance, believing that everyone is paying more attention to their appearance than they are.

The most challenging part of this stage for parents and teachers is defiant, but usually normal behavior, and the unbelievable rejection of adult standards. Ironically or perhaps comically, adolescents value the opinion of adults. Remember? We "oldies" experienced and survived adolescence and now can easily remember emulating adults during this stage. Some of these emulations were not positive, even dangerous. We all can recall adolescent friends who never made it to their twenty-first birthday. As former adolescents and now as parents, teachers and school leaders, we know the importance of guidance and direction from responsible adults.

During the middle years, rapid growth occurs. There is a shift in hormone production that affects metabolism, body growth, and sexual maturation. This may be the real reason we have physical education for boys and physical education for girls. Temporary physical awkwardness may occur at this developmental stage, especially for males.

Not only is the transition period destructive to self-esteem, but the adolescent also fluctuates between hyperactivity and lethargy as metabolism varies. Voice changes and growth of pubic hair are two major changes occurring during this stage. Most adolescents become more self-conscious at this time. We know that adolescent students hate to get up early, and according to several reputable studies, students would benefit if classes started later. Most middle school and high school classes begin before 8:00 AM.

In many middle schools, students are taught by teacher teams and individually monitored in teacher-student advisement periods. The middle school curriculum expresses a concern for the development of the individual child so that he or she can cope with the high school environment. In middle schools, students first began to change classes and receive instruction from several teachers on a daily basis.

The middle school is considered to be a place where adolescents can function in the appropriate learning environment by placing a special emphasis on the young adolescent or "preadolescent learner" between the ages of 10 and 15 (Queen 1999, 189).

The major purpose of the high school is to prepare students for the adult world of college or work. High schools are usually departmentalized, and are considered to be the place where all hard work surmounts. Students are often challenged by demanding and stimulating curricula (The Smith Report, 2000). At the high school level, students are expected to take specific courses and they must graduate within a four-year period. There are many course offerings at the high school level ranging from an array of electives to numerous AP courses leading to possible college credit.

During the high school years, students have many opportunities to participate in various high school programs like football, basketball, band, and drama productions, in addition to many additional curricula activities. During this level of education, students are required to hold certain grade-point averages to participate in extra-curricular activities.

High school students become increasingly independent even as they continue to seek social acceptance. Their physical maturation during these years results in greater size, dexterity, and strength. They develop a clearer definition of their identity and their role in society, and they begin to formulate life ambitions and goals (Dugger 2000).

As educators, it is important to remember that it is the responsibility of the schools to educate students with the essential skills and strategies necessary for them to become informed, productive citizens in a democratic society. Schools must be designed to reflect the needs of society, to even impact society. Express to students that they are important, what they do in school is important, and that their contributions to society are important (Sternberg 2000). Duke (1999) reminds us that both the middle school and the high school are wonderful networks of advanced learning environments.

The Negative Consequences of the Eighth- to Ninth-Grade Transition

Environmental, educational, and social factors affect students making a transition from middle to high school. This transition could fit into the parameters of what Bloom (1978) describes as a "transitional life event." A transitional life event is unique in its nature and process, and occurs when substantial changes occur in one's environment. How one interacts with the new environment, and how dramatically different the new environment is from the previous environment influences one's reaction to the transition. An individual's personality, resources, skills, and perceptions affect the response to a new situation (Reyes, Gillock, Kobus, and Sanchez 2000).

The substance of the high school environment has a dramatic impact on the social structure of the transitioning student. Typically, the new student is entering a much more heterogeneous student body encompassed by a more complex organizational and social structure. The personality of the student, along with attitude and disposition, will determine whether this new environment will be viewed as a challenge or an overwhelming event. The student peer relationships, established at the middle school level, are in a state of flux during the same period students are trying to adapt to a new social order. In addition, students report that there is less school-based social support at the high school level (Midgley, Eccles, and Feldlaufer 1991).

Combined with the environmental and social changes, students must adapt to rising educational standards. Grading, instructional practices, and departmentalization differ at the high school level. Often, expectations of the students are higher and maintaining former performance levels increases in difficulty. Inadequate planning and staff development in block scheduling have added new dimensions to these concerns. (Midgely et al. 1991; Queen 2000). These factors are consistent with the findings that the grades of students fall when transitioning into ninth grade. In addition, these grade changes have been linked to students who ultimately drop out of high school. The greater degree in which grades drop after the transition, the more likely the student will quit school (Roderick

1993). The point of vulnerability in student success is during the transition to a new school level.

The Impact of the Dropout on the Individual and Society

School administrators cannot ignore the importance of identifying potential school dropouts at the earliest opportunity. The National Center for Educational Statistics (1996) reports that in 1994, 12 percent of 16-24 year-olds had not completed high school. Of this number, eight percent were white, 13 percent African American, and 30 percent Latino. These numbers can also be disaggregated by urban, rural, and suburban youths: urban students dropping out at a rate of 8.9 percent; rural students at 6.8 percent; and suburban youths at 5.4 percent (U.S. Department of Education, National Center for Educational Statistics 1996).

Students who drop out of high school experience lifelong difficulties. Among these difficulties is disenfranchisement from society, poor mental health, a greater likelihood of entering low-paying jobs, and unemployment. These factors are more pronounced for youth from minority and low-income backgrounds (Reyes et al. 2000). In addition, the number of Hispanic youths in the United States is rapidly increasing.

The economic outlook of these youths can be quantified. In 1990, the median earnings of adult men between the ages of 25 and 34 who dropped out of school were 35 percent less than those who earned a high school diploma. Males who earned a college diploma earned twice as much. The figures are similar for women. Female dropouts earned 40 percent less than their high school counterparts and their average earnings were 65 percent lower than female college graduates (Roderick 1993). These figures suggest that school officials must be aware of the indicators that affect the likelihood of a student dropping out. Schools cannot be considered successful if they fail to maintain an environment that incorporates the developmental needs of all students.

Dropping out of school is defined as the "act of rejecting membership in a community in which youths feel marginal, gain little self-esteem, perceive few rewards, and which they also experience as rejecting them" (Anderson, Jacobs, Schramm, and Splittgerber 2000, 329). Research provides evidence that during the transition period, many students drop out of school, and their grades tend to suffer to some degree. Research states that by the tenth grade, as many as 6 percent of the students had dropped out of school (Mizelle 1999). However, when middle school students took part in a high school transition program, there was a decrease in the dropout rate. This occurred because the schools provided supportive advisory group activities and responsive remediation programs.

During the transition from middle to senior high school, there are an exceeding number of students who elect to drop out of school. Students that are identified as at-risk students are those who have a high probability of failing to complete the high school level (Messick and Reynolds 1992).

Principals identified these students as those frequently sent to the office, those with infrequent attendance, those who move around, girls who elect to live with boyfriends, and those who get in trouble with the justice system. Reasons for the decision to drop out of school vary from student to student.

Rates were higher for students who made the transition at the tenth-grade level as opposed to the seventh-grade level. He also discovered that boys dropped out more than girls, and that most students dropped out of school more frequently in the eleventh grade regardless of the year of transition (Alspaugh 2000).

Many students experience a time when keeping up with school-work becomes an extremely difficult task, and instead of resolving the issue, many students decide to drop out of school. These problems tend to occur during a transitional year. These problems may include social issues or insufficient academic performance. In some cases, the students are able to cope with this issue with very little assistance, but in extreme cases parents and teachers may need to intervene. Several common indicators are listed in Table 1.

When one or more of these attributes characterizes an adolescent, the student will likely need assistance from both the classroom teacher(s) and the parents to successfully complete his or her educational experience. Stepping back and allowing the student to attempt to figure it out on his own is not a just remedy and usually leads to extreme failure within the school environment (Robertson 1997).

Table 1. Common Indicators of At Risk Students

- Constant attention problems as a young child
- Multiple retentions in grade
- Poor grades
- Constant absenteeism
- Lack of connection with the school
- Behavior problems
- Lack of confidence
- Limited goals for the future

Responding to a Rapidly Changing National and Global Society

Any attempt to understand the impact of student transitions from middle to high school must be understood against the backdrop of the larger socio-economic changes affecting our students and our schools alike. Changes in the national economy are raising the economic stakes for students who underachieve or drop out of school. As the stakes rise, demands for education reform, higher standards, and stringent accountability are increasing pressure on schools and students. For students already buffeted by the physiological turbulence of adolescence, rising economic stakes and concomitant stress of ever-increasing academic expectations threaten to push some to the brink of giving up. Although as school leaders we have little control over socio economic forces, it is imperative that we develop policies aimed at fostering positive and effective school transitions to ensure that students stay in school and that they learn the skills and knowledge necessary to function in society.

Today's post-modernist, post-industrial society demands high levels of academic achievement and equally high levels of educational attainment. Although a precise definition of post-modernism is illusive (Halsey, Lauder, Brown, and Wells 1997), there is little doubt that we live in what can be framed as a post-modern society.

In its celebration of rugged individualism and individual rights, American society has always been characterized by a hint of modernity, but the degree of fragmentation, pluralism, and individualism—the atomization of society into sub-cultures—is unparalleled in American history. This fragmentation, coupled paradoxically with the rise of global telecommunication technologies, is reshaping institutions, including schools.

A prominent feature of a post-modern society is the rise of the information-based economy. Unlike its industrial and agrarian predecessors, the information-based economy places a premium on knowledge. Knowledge, of course, has always been a source of power. However, in an era in which the acquisition, synthesis, and distribution of information and information-based services has displaced manufacturing as the dominate engine of the economy, the rise of what Reich calls the "symbolic analysts—those in the media, law, finance, science and technology, education, and other professions (Reich 1997)—has subordinated, if not displaced, low-skilled, blue-collar labor" (Halsey et al. 1997).

As noted by Brown & Lauder (1997): "[the] view that the future wealth of nations will depend on the exploitation of leading-edge technologies, corporate innovation, and *the upgrading of the quality of human resources* [emphasis added] can hardly be quarreled with" (p. 180). Increased globalization and the rapid expansion of low-cost telecommunications technologies have combined to internationalize economies, resulting in the erosion of national economic boundaries. The result, according to Reich, (1997) is that the economic boats of what he calls redundant and in-person service workers have sprung leaks and are sinking. Moreover, even middle-level management jobs, particularly those associated with redundant production typical of hierarchical corporations operating within post-industrial and Fordist economies (Brown and Lauder 1997), are being displaced as routine jobs are being moved to Asia, Central America, and South America. By contrast, symbolic analysts are prospering. Possessing the knowledge and skills most needed in the information-based, technologically driven economies of the West and in parts of Asia, the symbolic analysts are able to auction their knowledge and skills to the highest bidder. They are also able to transfer their skills to multiple markets and to diverse industries, thereby creating substantial social and economic security for themselves and their families.

Consequently, the benefits of economic globalization and the rapid development of new technologies are unevenly distributed. Aronowitz and De Fazio (1997) posit that a significant gap is growing between intellectual, technical, and manual labor. Put another way, there is a widening economic polarization between highly skilled labor and deskilled labor. The result is a growing economic and social disparity between the intellectual haves and the intellectual have-nots—a type of cognitive-gap or cognitive-segregation that elevates a few and marginalizes the many.

This development is not theoretical; it is already having a malevolent impact on those who do not possess the skills demanded in an information economy. Neef (1998) reports that the trend toward the polarization of earnings is increasingly evident in Western economies:

> Never before the 1990s has the U.S. economy experienced broad, real-wage reductions among the majority of its workforce—even while the economy continued to grow. The hardest hit have been people with low levels of education or skills, those blue-collar workers who between 1973 and 1993 found real hourly wages dropping between 15 percent and 19 percent. (p. 9)

He notes that the age of Americans falling below the poverty level rose 50 percent from 1979 to 1992 and that the benefits of the new economy are going to knowledge workers who comprise 20 percent of the population, but who earn more than four-fifths of the workforce combined.

As a result, the impact of dropping out of school can be devastating. According to Hauser (1997), as of 1992, 87 percent of 19 to 20 year-olds have completed high school. The disaggregated data reveal that high school completion rates are 91 percent for whites, 81 percent for African Americans, and 65 percent for Hispanics. Moreover, as would be expected, employment varies directly with high school completion. Since 1970, the differential in employment rates between high school graduates and dropouts has grown steadily (reflecting the emergence of the information-economy). Employment has been very high and stable among college graduates, while it has declined among high school graduates, and especially high school dropouts. Employment for women has increased among all women, including dropouts, but the growth has been greater for female high school and college graduates. By the early 1990's, a college woman was at least ten age points more likely to work outside the home than was a male dropout. Hauser (1997) observes that:

> Just as the earning power of high school graduates has declined relative to that of college students, so has the earning power of high school dropouts fallen relative to that of high school graduates. Indeed, the economic consequences of dropping out of high school have never been so severe. Over the past two decades, the earnings of white male dropouts declined from 85 percent to less than 75 percent of earnings relative to high school graduates. Among African American and Hispanic men there is evidence of a decline in the earnings of dropouts relative to high school graduates. (p. 154)

Failure to complete high school has more than economic effects; it marginalizes individuals both politically and socially. For example, Hauser (1997) reports that "electoral participation by high school dropouts is less than among high school graduates," continues to observe that "failure to obtain at least a high school diploma looks more and more like the contemporary equivalent of functional illiteracy. High school dropout indicates a failure to pass minimum thresholds of economic, social, or political motivation, access, and competence" (p. 154).

What is the role of education in addressing the new economic realities and the attending economic and social disparities? If, as Brown and Lauder (1997) point out, "knowledge, learning, information, and technical competence are the new raw materials of international commerce," then schools have a major role to play ensuring that students have the requisite knowledge and skills to contribute to and benefit from the new information economy of the twenty-first century. Failure to provide students with a world-class education will condemn all but the most privileged to the bottom rung of the economic ladder. In his provocative essay, *An Era of Man-Made Brainpower Industries* (1991), Lester Thurow warns that:

> With the ability to make anything anywhere in the world and sell it anywhere else in the world, business firms can 'cherry pick' the skilled...wherever they exist in the world. Some third-world countries are now making massive investments in basic education. American firms don't have to hire an American high school graduate if that graduate is not world-class. His or her educational defects are not their problem. Investing to give the necessary market skills to a well-educated Chinese high school graduate may well look like a much more attractive investment (less costly) than having to retrain...a poorly trained American high school graduate. (Neef 1998)

Education, then, has a crucial role to play in preparing the nation's children to compete in a global, post-modern economy—knowledge is indispensable for economic survival. Gone are the days when a student could graduate from high school and expect to obtain life-long gainful employment. Now, students need a post-high school education and a commitment to life-long learning if they are to share in the prosperity of the American economy. Although researchers debate the degree to which educational attainment and economic status are causally linked, the literature indicates that education level can account for up to "60 percent of variance in adult occupational status" (Halsey et al. 1997, 35).

In short, students need a high degree of functional literacy as well as strong communication, interpersonal, technical, and problem-solving skills. Such skills transcend the vagaries of economic expansion and retraction and give students highly marketable and adaptive skills that can be employed across a wide spectrum of industries and economic conditions.

The dilemma facing school leaders is how to prepare students for the increased intellectual demands of the information-economy without increasing the academic pressure to the point of forcing already marginalized students out of school. This is a particularly acute problem for urban school districts with large populations of at-risk students and marginalized populations.

The plight of inner-city urban schools is largely invisible to professional educators, most of who are middle class and white. Although theoretically aware of the social, economic, and educational devastation of inner-city schools, public citizen's general knowledge and perceptions are pale reflections of the harsh realities of these schools. Jean Anyon (1999) goes a long way toward awakening a deeper understanding and, one would hope moral indignation, at the plight of inner-city children.

Anyon begins by drawing into sharp relief the disparity between urban and suburban schools. He reports that only 29 percent of the nation's population lives in our central cities, whereas 48 percent of the U.S. population resides in the suburbs. Because suburban voters represent a higher age of the population and turn out for elections in higher numbers than urban voters, they hold considerably more political power than inner city residents do. The result is the political isolation of the inner cities. This political isolation manifests itself in concentrated poverty (40 percent of urban students attend high poverty schools, whereas only 10 percent of suburban students attend high poverty schools) and in large funding disparities. According to Anyon, "despite greater need, 79% of large city districts studied by the Council of the Great City Schools are funded at a lower rate than are suburban schools; nationally, advantaged suburban schools spend as much as ten times that spent by urban poor schools" (p. 7). Urban schools are also plagued by relatively poor instruction; the instruction is characterized by limited access to math and science resources and programs, and is based on "cognitively low-level, unchallenging, rote material."

The combined effects of a changing economy, demands for higher standards and accountability, and the marginalization of urban schools create an educational environment in which students from middle- and upper-class families with adequate supplies of material, social, and culture capital thrive successfully. However, a large number of at-risk students underachieve at best, or worse, give up on a system ill prepared to meet their academic and social needs.

School administrators cannot solve the deeply entrenched socio-economic disparities in society, nor can they shelter students from the increasing demands of the information age. However, they can work to create school cultures that ease students through the turbulent adolescent years and that effectively transition them from the middle to the high school experience. Although a multifaceted approach to preventing school dropout and underachievement is necessary, more attention needs to be focused upon creating smooth transitions from middle to high school. Healthy transitions will facilitate academic and social assimilation and increase the likelihood that students will stay in school and will learn.

Student Concerns During Transitions

What does it mean to be prepared? Prior to the transition, a female student had numerous opportunities to visit her new high school. During these visits, she was given tours that followed her schedule, thus making it easier for her to get from class to class, and she had the opportunity to practice opening her locker. The student also had the chance to meet her teachers, the guidance counselor, and the school administrator and was informed of the expectations that they had at the high school level. She received a student handbook and her parents received an information packet.

To make this transition even easier, the student was assigned a buddy who assisted in helping the new student move from class to class and provided answers to questions that focused on high school standards. The student developed a higher level of confidence, because she was prepared for the impending change and she approached the situation with an open mind, because she was familiar with her new environment (Shoffner and Williamson 2000).

In an all too familiar situation, there was a separate case in which there was no level of preparedness evident. A male student had a negative experience because he was not prepared to enter the big high school. In contrast to the previous situation, this student was not familiar with his classes or schedule and spent most of his time wandering in the hallway and arriving to class late. The student also experienced difficulty attempting to open his locker, and had no clue of the expectations of his teachers, the school administrator, or the guidance counselor. The student left his first day at the big school feeling inadequate, ill prepared, and unsure of direction.

There are many issues surrounding the transition process from the middle school to the senior high school. The students have several concerns that they express, as do their parents. In this section, there are explanations concerning strategies that can help ease the transition.

As students make the transition from middle school to high school, they have many concerns. In a survey that was compiled during middle school, students were asked to share their thoughts and feelings about going to the high school. Their responses were: "I'm afraid I'll get lost.", "Will I fit in?", "I might fail.", and "What if they taunt me?"(Capelluti and Stokes 1991, 19). Overall, there was a continued expression of fear, anxiety, uncertainty, and confusion. It is evident that many students are extremely fearful of attending the big high school.

This fear surfaces because students have not had the opportunity to visit the school and they don't know what to expect; therefore, they develop a personal perception that attending the big high school is scary and that the teachers are mean and that they will have mountains of homework assignment to complete with very little guidance.

In the survey, many students expressed a concern for failure. They viewed the "big school" as a place that would surpass their levels of knowledge. Because of the lack of exposure to the high school, many middle school students were unsure of the expectations of the teachers. They did not think that they could go to the teacher to ask questions pertaining to specific assignments.

The middle school students also expressed a concern of making new friends. They viewed the high school as a place that would destroy long-time friendships, and they would be forced to make new friends. During this level of transition, there seems to be a major concern for success and acceptance. The students want a circle of friends, and they want to be accepted by that circle of friends (Rossi and Stokes 1991). Additional concerns are identified in Table 2.

Table 2. Student Concerns About Transitioning

- Concerned about getting to class on time, finding lockers, dealing with crowded hallways, and getting lost
- Afraid they will be picked on, teased, or victimized by other students
- Concerned about being safe in the new school
- Concerned with understanding difficult courses
- Concerned about rigid rules and strict teachers
- Difficulty making new friends in a new setting

Parental Concerns During Transitions

When students leave the middle school to enter the high school, parents have justifiable concerns. The concerns tend to center on academics. During this period, parents also have to make a change. For instance, they were once heavily involved in the elementary and the middle schools, but once their child reaches the high school level, there tends to be less parental involvement because students are not comfortable with their parents around. On the positive end, many parents choose to remain involved during the high school years, and research shows that students whose parents are involved in the education process have a tendency to do better in their academics. The additional parental concerns are: 1) anonymity, 2) curriculum, and 3) safety.

Many parents are extremely intimidated by the size of the new school and they are very fearful that their child may "fall through the cracks,"(Williamson and Johnston 1999). They are afraid that their child will be placed in a classroom where a teacher pays very little attention to the needs of the child, and most parents really have a problem with the school's lack of continual contact.

The curriculum is problematic for many parents. They view the curriculum as a maze of unconnected activities and are confused by content. They feel that if they as parents can't comprehend the curriculum, neither will the child.

Safety, sociability, and civility are elements that all parents want for their children. They want reassurance that their child will be safe in the learning environment, and they have concerns about student behavior. Furthermore, they feel that schools tolerate high levels of rude behavior, and that there should be zero tolerance for rudeness and incivility. They also want their child to have the opportunity to socialize during given times.

It is extremely important for parents to be involved in the learning process, even at the high school level. Mizelle (1999) points out many strategies that have been proven to help parents assist their child during the learning process at the high school level; students experience higher levels of achievement, become better adjusted, and are less prone to drop out of school.

This involvement at the high school level is encouraged through a variety of activities. For instance, parents can participate in conferences with their child and the guidance counselor to analyze coursework and generate schedules, make visits to the learning facility during the spring or fall, spend a day observing the high school environment, and assist in designing and facilitating activities for students. Contrary to popular belief, a parent's level of involvement in the learning process really does make a difference in a student's academic success.

2

The Role of Educators Must Change

In *Global Trends 2005: An Owner's Manual for the Next Decade* (1999), Michael Mazarr asserts that we are living amid change, traveling out of the industrial era and into the era of knowledge at a rapid pace. Society is transforming the focus from the building of things to the manipulating of information, emphasizing process over product, and valuing relationships over differences. Mazarr highlights education as a lifelong process rather than a one-time event in today's world. Thus, the changing roles of educators evolves around the goal of developing life-long learners who are adaptable to a rapidly transforming workplace rather than preparing a student for a specific job or career.

Education at the federal level reflects the impact of the knowledge era by raising the learning standards for all children and supporting efforts to improve schools that serve minority and impoverished children. As Secretary of Education, Rod Paige intends to spread a culture of accountability throughout the Department of Education (Sack 2001). As state governors feel an increasing degree of pressure in answering for the level of academic performance among their states' schools, they are demanding more power over school districts. The number of governors who name their state school superintendents, as well as the state board members, is on the rise, as is their control over education monies. Ironically, while the bureaucracy appears to be tightening from the top, the trend at the local level is to empower front-line workers in the decision-making process. With the implementation of high-stakes testing and the dropout rate on the rise, educators are faced with the dilemma of focusing efforts on passing the test or providing meaningful student learning experiences. Wagner & Vander Ark (2001) believe that rebuilding an accountability system that measures the production of quality student work addresses both the issues of accountability and the demands of the Knowledge Era. Presently, a blurring of the boundaries in professional roles at the school site are evolving in response to accountability mandates at local, state and national levels.

The Role of the Central Office

The role of the central office staff, reported by Robert Johnston (2001), is to be one of the most under utilized resources available in local school efforts to improve student achievement. Central office staff and their connection to raising student achievement has recently become a topic of discussion and research in school administration preparation programs. While principals certainly should possess at least one area of instructional expertise, they cannot be experts in all areas. Central office staff can provide the missing knowledge and skills at the school sites. Central office personnel should be astute at aligning the budget to address the needs of the instructional program. In addition, the instructional program should be driven by data disaggregations. Finally, school districts should behave more aggressively in "growing their own" effective leaders by providing leadership training opportunities for promising employees. At present, a model school district does not exist. While some districts contain some high performing schools, no districts possess a consistent high level of performance among all the schools (Johnston 2001). The answer to this inconsistency may lie with the local school level administrator.

The Role of the Principal

The principal is the most important person during the transition period at the school. In addition to handling everyday situations, the principal must establish guidelines that will assist in making the transition easier. Not only must those guidelines be established, the principal needs to make sure that those guidelines are being followed. As the leader at the school, the principal needs to be proactive in advocating the necessary changes that will ensure an easier transition for students. It is the duty of the principal to delegate responsibilities to other staff members, or a transition team, who will play a vital role during the process. This can be initiated by attempting to establish and maintain a working relationship between the middle school and high school principals. Together, these principals and their transition teams should hold information sessions about transitions. During the sessions, they should make it a point to address parental issues concerning the transition process.

The role of principal is transforming, as is reflected by the alternative training programs being implemented across the nation. Preparation for school administration has centered on structured internship experiences in which reflective practices and a commitment to transforming schools is developed. "As new accountability measures take effect, a broad consensus has emerged in education policy circles that raising the quality of school leadership is essential" (Keller 2000). Thus, the 1980's concept of the "instructional leader" is reshaped by the accountability mantra. "Principals, instead of being building managers, should become leaders of instruction—dynamic, inspirational educators focused almost exclusively on raising student achievement" (Olsen 2000).

What exactly does "instructional leadership" look like? An instructional leader might be an individual who spends a large amount of time in the classrooms with the students and the teachers. An instructional leader might coordinate instructional materials, time, and staff to support instructional goals. An instructional leader should be the motivating force within a school building. An instructional leader must know what it takes to improve student achievement. However, in addition to student achievement, a principal is also accountable for running the buses, feeding the children, and maintaining a safe and orderly environment. Olsen (2000) states that principals who are effective at leading instruction must possess the ability to nurture others into sharing the leadership role. Principals must possess leadership content knowledge and practice distributed leadership. An effective administrator will build leadership capacity among the faculty based on the strengths of individuals. Ultimately, the role of the principal as instructional leader is to nurture the leadership abilities of classroom teachers as a means of improving instruction and raising student achievement. Burnham (2001) has found in a study of recent principal graduates that the training they received in university preparatory programs had become more focused on instructional leadership. He builds the case that universities must prepare their principal graduates to be ready to be leaders of student achievement.

Classroom Teachers as Instructional Leaders

In "New Roles Tap Expertise of Teachers," Jeff Archer (2001) identifies four types of instructional teacher-leaders: the staff development teacher, the lead teacher, the peer assistance and review teacher, and the consulting teacher. Each type of teacher-leader is empowered to assist in improving classroom instruction in specific ways. The staff development teacher works with colleagues to identify instructional areas needing improvement and design staff development opportunities to address those needs. This person visits classrooms and works in a coaching manner to facilitate quality instruction; however, the staff development teacher does not report observational data concerning particular teachers' abilities to the administration. The staff development teacher works to improve staff development throughout the school. The lead teacher functions in more of an administrative capacity; i.e., assisting in the hiring of new teachers. The peer-assistance-and-review teacher is "empowered to police" the teachers, providing recommendations as to who keeps their jobs and who does not. The consulting teacher leaves the classroom to help other teachers be successful. This teacher-leader also participates in the evaluation process of their colleagues. After three years, the consulting teacher returns to the classroom (Archer 2001). The success of these positions relies heavily on the principal's ability to select and train the appropriate teachers to serve in leadership capacities and on the professionalism and commitment of the staff.

Classroom Teachers as Agents of Socialization

In some respects, teachers have always served as a socializing force in their students' lives. However, the demands on teachers to provide socialization for children have become more encompassing and more complex as varied family backgrounds, cultural diversity, language and learning barriers, and mass media exposure inundate the lives of children. Typically, the younger the student the greater the expectation that the teacher will function as a socialization force within the school setting. Elementary teachers spend a large portion of time instructing children on the student role. As a child moves through the grades and into high school, Good and Brophy (2000) report that socialization is dealt with through administration or other support personnel. However, at every level "teachers need to develop knowledge and strategies for meeting students' [social-emotional] needs, not just to foster these students' social-emotional adjustment, but also to enable them to make satisfactory academic progress" (184). For this reason, some high schools have elected to create "school-within-a-school" structures that personalize teacher efforts at continuing to positively impact the socialization of students as they move through adolescence and into adulthood.

Roles of Educators in Transitioning Students to High School

As previously stated, one of the most critical times for educators to be most sensitive to the socialization of students is during the transition from middle school to high school. Until recently, small efforts have been made to smooth out this difficult time for adolescents. In the age of accountability and with several of the standardized tests falling at the ninth-grade level, more attention is being paid to this transitional period. Table 3 compares the roles of various educators dealing with transitions. Educators today must not only educate students in reading, writing, and arithmetic but must also equip students with the motivation and skills to continue learning beyond the walls of the school. As the world becomes increasingly more competitive and technology expands information and communication horizons, students must be more diverse and flexible in their ability to adapt and grow as employees and citizens. In such a rapidly changing society, school remains one of the key socializing forces in American culture. Educators must continue to redefine and expand upon their roles as they shape young people to meet the needs of tomorrow's world.

Table 3. Roles of Educators in Transitioning Students from Middle to High School

County Office Staff	School Principals	Classroom Teachers
Provide an overview of transitional programs, designing a general format for the school district to follow.	Set the success of all freshman students as a top priority for the school.	Build a team atmosphere among the ninth-grade teachers in relation to behavior, academics, and extra-curricular events.
Coordinate plans and mediate issues between the feeder school and the receiving school.	Make scheduling and facility decisions with the needs of ninth graders in mind.	Cultivate appropriate personal relationships with students.
Provide support through training, materials and time.	Select and motivate quality teachers to teach the ninth-grade classes.	Be proactive in establishing supportive parental relationships.
	Provide staff development opportunities based on the needs of the freshman teachers.	Communicate with both the middle school and upperclassman teachers to create a seamless transition from middle school to high school.
	Investigate alternative behavior management plans that meet the needs of the ninth-grade students .	Seek the assistance of support personnel when a student does not appear to be handling transition successfully.
	Actively participate in the county transitional program, working closely with the administration at the feeder/receiving school.	
	Involve parents in the transition phase early.	

Teachers Can Provide Direct Assistance

I believe that there must be direct, meaningful teacher involvement during the transition stage. When schools are responsive to the needs of educators who facilitate instruction, the education process in conjunction with the transition phase can improve significantly. The staff also needs to be armed with skills that make the transition easier, and a clear understanding of the characteristics of the cognitive, social, and emotional development. In fact, when students make the transition from the middle school to the high school, there is a need for staff members to understand and accept the students regardless of their varying backgrounds.

It is the duty of the teacher to continue to encourage the student. This is a time when students become vulnerable and self-esteem is extremely low. At this point, the student tends to seek guidance and assurance. Encourage the incoming students to always do their best work and to avoid peer pressure. Students need to be accepted for who they are, but they also need guidance and support. During the adolescent years, students' self-esteem is insufficient, and their egos may be delicate, therefore, it is important to continue to express encouragement, praise and recognition for any task.

We, as professional educators, can demonstrate support by attending events after school, and by advising the student to always put forth his or her best effort. Teachers can also show support by assisting the student with homework assignments or projects that are school related. We must never forget that students need to be actively engaged in the learning process.

Freshmen come from a variety of environments, some which were much smaller in comparison to the high school. Some students may have been taught by a team of four or five teachers, often in an interdisciplinary fashion, as opposed to six or seven different teachers. It is also important to remember that all students have different socio-economic backgrounds.

What can be done to ease the transition from the middle school to the "big school" known as the high school? The possibilities are immense, and these strategies have been proven to work at many different facilities. Earlier in the chapter, there was a declaration that transition from the middle school to the high school could be a very stressful moment for many young adolescents; therefore, many researchers emphasize valuable points to making the transition as smooth as possible. A smooth transition requires both communication and a strong relationship between the staff of both facilities (McElroy 2000).

In the following section, I discuss a few strategies that have worked in schools thereby making the transition easier for students.

Strategies Teachers Can Consider Using

Strategies to consider include a range of meetings focusing on course requirements, parent information meetings, individual conferences, mentoring, career counseling, peer mediation groups and other school presentations.

Throughout the research, I have discovered several different approaches to easing the transition from middle to senior high school. Below is a suggested list for smoothing the transition for students, and by utilizing these methods, students become less apprehensive about beginning high school. Hertzog and Morgan (1997), who authored the article "From Middle School to High School," recommended these strategies in *Easing the Transition* (1997).

- Provide eighth-grade students with guidance sessions that are led by ninth-grade guidance counselors during the spring/fall to discuss the high school curriculum, registration, and scheduling. This is also a good time to discuss expectations and responsibilities. A booklet or pamphlet detailing the information may be helpful at this time.

- Hold a "parent night" at the high school to discuss the curriculum, scheduling, and co-curricular activities. Once again, this is a good time to include parents by detailing expectations at the high school level and noting the responsibilities of the incoming freshman.

- Organize an eighth-grade field trip to the new high school.

- Develop a "transition team" composed of middle-level and high school teachers. They should meet on a monthly basis to plan and conduct a transition activities schedule for the school year.

- Institute an advisor/advisee program in the high school.

- Coordinate ongoing pen pal relationships between middle and high school students.

- Organize a "Teacher Swap-a-Day" where high school teachers teach eighth-grade students and middle school teachers teach ninth-grade students.

- Develop a program where students, faculty, and administrators can "shadow" someone for a day.

- Hold celebrations that signify the end of the middle level and the beginning of the high school experience.

- Plan an information fair (carnival like) to disseminate information related to the high school curriculum, academics, vocational offerings, electives, and course offerings.

- Offer an eighth-grade exploratory session that provides students the opportunity to analyze the connections between academic subjects and careers.

- Allot time for the high school department chairs or high school students to visit the middle schools to discuss the life of high school students.

- Encourage ninth-grade subject area teachers to review eighth-grade student portfolios.

- Arrange for high school faculty members, counselors, and parents to work together to develop a five-year plan for seventh-graders.

- Develop ninth-grade teams to aid in the transition.

Effective transition programs devised to guide students and parents step-by-step will ensure that the first week of school will be calmer and better organized. During open house, which should be held early first semester, parents complete evaluations concerning the transitional period, and the staff uses the data to make recommended changes.

A Successful Transition

For students to make successful transitions, they must be well prepared. In terms of having a successful transition, there are two different approaches recommended: preparedness and support. (Anderson, Jacobs, Schramm, and Splittgerber 2000).

- *Academic Preparedness:* It is pertinent that students possess skills that are necessary for them to succeed at the next level

- *Independence and Industriousness:* Students need to be able to work independently, and remain on task with very little teacher supervision

- *Conformity to Adult Standards:* Students who "conform to adult standards of behavior and effort" are better able to adjust to the next school level

- *Coping Mechanisms:* Allows students to deal with problems and difficulties they are likely to encounter upon transition to the next school level. These tactics include attaining necessary information, ways to keep up with multiple assignments, and ways to effectively resolve conflicts. Students who posses effective coping mechanisms tend to be more successful in making the transition from one school level to the next.

Support from others is another important aspect in making a successful transition from one level to the next level. The researchers in this study have identified four different types of support: informational, tangible, emotional, and social. Informational support encompasses levels of knowledge, for example knowing what to expect. Tangible refers to "provision of resources or services" (331). Emotional emphasizes a clear understanding of the emotional needs of adolescent learners, and social involves having friends in the same school setting. Regardless of the situation, parents, peers, and teachers can provide support. There is much evidence that suggest that various levels of support are effective during the transition period.

- Students from environments that express levels of support experience less academic difficulty as they progressed through the transition. This was evident through the degree in which parents and children participated together in non-school activities.

- Teachers who were more accessible to students at the next level facilitated successful school transitions. Just making themselves available to the students showed levels of concern and support.

- Having friends who help students cope with transition related concerns are another form of support.

- Students benefit when a transition team (consisting of counselor, teachers, and students) is in place to help them understand the academic rigor and co-curricular options.

- Simply providing students with information about the transition can help them can help them through the transition phase.

Parents, teachers, and guidance counselors play a major role in the lives of students. They hold the key in determining whether the transition stage is easier or difficult for students who are approaching that stage in life. Once again, there are strategies that parents and teachers can utilize in managing the transition process.

In a previous section, there was a discussion concerning parents who have students entering the high school. In this section, there will be an attempt to address those concerns by developing a level of parental awareness. To develop a level of awareness with parents is to (a) start a dialogue with the community, (b) stop explaining, (c) talk about achievement, (d) ensure planned community relations, and (e) work for a civil environment (Williamson and Johnston 1999).

Instead of allowing parents to develop their own personal views of the school and its programs, initiate a dialogue between the school and the parents. Share the commitments of the school and creating a cohesive group of parents and educators to review and analyze the school's mission in relation to established programs.

Confront the issue and work toward solutions so that there can be a level of awareness and support from parents and community members.

Stop explaining! Schools are often expected to explain everything. Explaining, defending, and rationalizing certain programs is perceived by parents as defensive. We as teachers and principals do too much of this! Furthermore, this type of discussion elicits confusion and inappropriate conclusions about intentions and levels of effectiveness can be confused. When there are concerns about program development and effectiveness, the committee of parents, teachers, and administrators should hold a meeting sharing the positive and negative aspects of the education program.

The third task for parental awareness is a discussion centering on academic achievement. Some parents believe that schools are not addressing the academic needs of their children. They are concerned about the curriculum, teaching methods, and the additional needs of the academically gifted. It is the job of the school to devise a plan to remedy any problem. Acknowledging weaknesses and then using these as opportunities for greater collaboration, is an effective method that enhances community and parental support. Invite parents to become partner in designing solutions.

In order to ensure planned community relations, schools should make themselves available. When children become older, it becomes extremely difficult to remain informed about the high school happenings. Some type of liaison or a transition panel or committee can be established to communicate with parents and community members about student needs. Schools must work with parents to identify information needs and design steps that will provide parents with valid and immediate responses (Williamson and Johnston 1999).

The fifth concern was to work for a civil environment. Many parents view the middle school as being out of control. Parents often view student behavior as dangerous and chaotic whereas middle school and high school teachers may view the behavior as a normal part of adolescent development.

Teachers have a pertinent role in the transition process from middle to senior high school. Paving the road for the adolescent's journey through high school is a task that is filled with ups and downs. It challenges every fiber of the successful teacher.

These suggestions have been helpful for high school teachers. For instance, teachers must know and understand the physical, social, and emotional characteristics of high school students, teachers should expect to be tested by adolescent students; therefore, as teachers, we should remain calm when being tested or challenged. Finally, teachers must express praise and recognition for adolescents to remain motivated about school, and teachers must realize that rising middle level students have a strong need for discipline and guidance.

Teachers recognize that a well-articulated program helps to provide a smooth transition from the middle level to the high school level, and they must be able to accommodate the differences that exist between beginning high school students and those preparing for graduation. These teachers provide numerous opportunities for students to participate in a variety of school related experiences, and they value the students regardless of their cultural, racial, or socioeconomic backgrounds and status, and they truly believe that all students can and will learn (Rossi and Stokes 1991).

Nine Principles to Abide By

McElroy (2000) offers nine principles for effective practices.

Principle 1. Each and every lesson should incorporate a kinesthetic activity that enhances the quality of learning.

Principle 2. Teachers must believe that every child has the ability to learn.

Principle 3. Learning should be an enticing and fundamental experience for both the student and the teacher.

Principle 4. Enhance programs by integrating the curriculum with other subject areas.

Principle 5. Curriculum should be taught through an interdisciplinary approach.

Principle 6. Music enhances curriculum studies.

Principle 7. Educators must be prepared to take a risk, and play the learner's role from time to time.

Principle 8. Administrators support teachers by displaying a level of trust, therefore it becomes the teacher's responsibility assess their levels of effectiveness.

Principle 9. A community of learners must be established beforehand.

3

Improving Transitions for Increased Student Achievement

Life for everyone is a series of transitions, some of which are traumatic and result in unhappiness and failure. Students transitioning between schools experience a range of emotions, from mild uncertainty and frustration to major anxiety and academic failure (Weldy 1991). Changing from middle to high school means changing buildings, encountering different expectations for learning, and moving from self-contained to departmentalized classes. Additionally, the school is larger, and the organization and schedule are more complex.

Murdock, Anderman, and Hodge (2000) claim that middle school is identified as a time of general academic risk. Student attitudes toward school become more negative; their self-esteem and academic self-concept decline; and they attribute waning value to academic endeavors. These behaviors associated with maladaptive motivational beliefs are good predictors that a student is at risk for not completing school. Students' experiences in middle school are predictive of their later motivation and behavior in high school. Expectancy-value theory emphasizes students' beliefs that they are capable of completing academic tasks. Self-concept models focus on students' more generalized sense of competence. These authors explain that work by Eccles and others emphasizes beliefs about the value of different tasks and the consonance between tasks and students' personal values. We know that motivation and achievement among early adolescents, including positive teacher-student relationships, supportive peer relationships, classroom and school goal orientation, and students' sense of belonging can be predictors of success. Students' school success has also been linked to their larger socioeconomic context; adolescents are less likely to achieve in school if they perceive limited relations between school and economic success.

As teachers we communicate information concerning the value of schooling and our expectations for students' success directly and tacitly through behaviors such as grading, goal setting, and feedback. Hence, various aspects of students' relationships with us are predictors of adolescents' motivation and ease of adaptation to school. High motivation among middle school students has been associated with teachers who know, support, challenge, and encourage them to act autonomously. Adolescents want to be taken seriously by their teachers. Positive student-teacher relationships are characterized by interpersonal warmth and by clearly communicating the value of students' academic learning and success. Studies of high school dropouts document poor relationships with teachers and perceived teacher disrespect/unfairness as central to students' decisions to leave school. Successful high school students reported that teachers pushed them to excel, whereas the less successful students saw teachers either as irrelevant or adversarial.

For some students, there may be negative social consequences for conforming to the values and behaviors desired by teachers when their peers discourage commitment to academic tasks. Ordinarily a correlation exists between students' own educational goals and aspirations, and the perceived and actual plans and expectations of their friends. Transitions between levels of schooling often bring with them a marked disruption in students' friendships as schools are consolidated and students are tracked into classrooms based on academic abilities. Thus, students become vulnerable to potentially negative peer influences during such transitions.

Beyond relationships and events that occur within school, students also receive information about the value of education from their observations of the larger world around them. Performing well in school may ensure future economic success, but some students' experiences contradict that proposition. Students, who are members of groups systematically underrepresented among well-paying professional careers, are apt to challenge the notion that education will guarantee future success. Student achievement was predicted by concrete rather than abstract values. Accordingly, students' perceptions of the economic value of educational success may influence their individual expectations and the degree to which they value academic achievement. (Murdock et al. 2000).

More Transitions Equal More Achievement Loss

In a 1998 study of 48 school districts, Alspaugh (1998) found that students involved in a pyramid transition of multiple elementary schools into a single middle school experienced a greater achievement loss than did students in a linear transition of a single elementary school to a middle school. Mixing students from multiple elementary schools in the transition tended to increase the transition achievement loss. Further, students attending middle schools experienced a greater achievement loss in the transition to high school than did the students making the transition from a K-8 elementary school. The experience of making a previous transition did not moderate the achievement loss during the transition to high school. Increased high school dropout rates for the students attending middle schools may have been associated with the achievement losses and the double transitions at grades six and nine. Moreover, recent researchers confirmed the loss of self-esteem and self-perception that other researchers previously found to be associated with school-to-school transitions. This loss may have been a contributing factor in the increased dropout rates found in this study. Students attending larger schools tended to experience more transitions than the students in smaller schools do, since schools with two transitions had higher dropout rates than schools with only one transition. Alspaugh's study paralleled findings of other researchers in that instability and adjustments required of students in school transitions are associated with educational outcomes. These findings imply that students placed in relatively small cohort groups for long spans of time tend to experience more desirable educational outcomes (Alspaugh 1998).

During the transition period, there is academic loss as determined by a decline in academic scores. For some reason or other, there is a drop in academic scores. This condition could exist for various reasons. Some influences of academic loss include social factors and emotional factors.

Reasons for Achievement Loss During the Transition

In many instances, students lose sight of their purpose or their academic goals, therefore, they tend to de-emphasize the importance of education. Sometimes, peers may influence them to develop a negative attitude towards school because they lack an understanding of the information being taught in the school setting. Because many students lack an understanding of the skills being taught, they are usually faced with embarrassment and ridicule. They withdraw from the school setting in order to avoid the cruel acts. The failure of the students to negotiate systematic transitions may initiate the gradual disengagement process from school, and promote conflict between the youth and the school as an institution, (Anderson, Jacobs, Schramm, and Splittgerber 2000).

Unfortunately, schools can become places that students do not wish to be; thus, they leave. Some indicators include increasing feelings of being anonymous, participation and leadership in extracurricular activities decrease, grades decline. In a separate survey students were asked to provide reasons why they decided to leave school, and 58 percent of boys and 44 percent of girls replied that they did not like school, and 46 percent of boys and 33 percent of girls were failing school. The smallest percentage included suspension in which 19 percent of boys and 13 percent of girls mentioned as a reason to quit school (Anderson, Jacobs, Schramm, and Splittgerber 2000).

Advice for Parents

It is important to remember that adolescents need their parents not just to establish what is deemed as appropriate expectations and boundaries but also to advocate and support them (Robertson

1997). Allowing the parent to become a part of the child's educational support team can ease this concern. Here is a list of additional strategies that

- Make time to listen to and attempt to understand the teen's fears/concerns
- Encouraging teen to participate in one or more school activities
- Attending school functions, sports and plays
- Providing a supportive home and school environment that clearly values education
- Emphasizing at home and in school the importance of study skills, hard work, and follow through
- Establishing appropriate boundaries for behavior that are constantly enforced

SUCCEED with troubled adolescents is a program devised to address issues concerning social, emotional, and learning (Dougherty, Greenspan, and Rodahan 1996). Educators using the program

- Collect information on the student prior to the beginning of the school year
- Develop a close home-school relationship
- Meet with the child
- Develop a program that would best suit the child
- Devise a tentative plan for dealing with problems
- Provide parents with ongoing feedback
- Demonstrate a caring attitude

The Relationship of Academic and Social Outcomes

When it comes to schooling, the academic outcomes of children and adolescents are highly related to their social outcomes (Juvonen and Wentzel 1996). MacIver and Epstein (1991) note that early adolescents are characterized by simultaneous and often conflicting needs. For example, adolescents need the security and support of close, caring adult supervision and guidance at the same time that they need increasing autonomy from adults. They need and want attention and recognition for their own unique abilities, successes, and achievements, but adolescents also want to be part of a crowd. They engage in the life-shaping process of self-exploration and self-definition while they need help in remedying their weaknesses and developing their strengths. Such help must be offered in a way that does not stigmatize them, label them, or separate them from their peers. Without support and guidance, some students flounder and fail and drop out of school.

Phelan, P, Davidson, A. & Cao, H. (1991) present students' *multiple worlds framework* that identifies four types of students. The framework focuses on adaptation strategies that students employ to transition between and adapt to different contexts and settings; i.e., students' abilities to transition successfully to school and classroom environments. Type I students experience worlds that are congruent and transition smoothly. Many, but not all, of these students are white, upper middle-class, and high achievers. These students experience tremendous pressure to achieve academically. They link achievement to long-range educational goals. Excessive pressure to achieve academically can result in unintended educational costs. For example, some students describe their emphasis as "learning to play the game" rather than learning to learn. Others report their inability or lack of inclination to remember content material following exams. Some students worry so much about their classroom performance that they obstruct their ability to concentrate. Moreover, some students report a decrease in their intrinsic interest to learn.

Academic stress has social and emotional costs as well. Preoccupation with grades can lead to competitive behavior with friends and sometimes leaves students with conflicting and troubling thoughts. Some students discuss the depression they experience after receiving less than perfect scores. Many schools do not have specific support to help students deal with excessive stress over grades and test scores.

Type II students are those with worlds very different but manage to "border cross" successfully. High achieving minority students frequently exhibit patterns common to this type. They report pressure to do well academically; but unlike Type I students, half of these young people express discomfort and stress in classes where they feel isolated and alone. They are often one of a few minority students in their high track classes. Fear of speaking up in class emanates from their perception of differential power relationships within the classroom context, as well as suspicion of knowledge of their classmates' prejudices. Their silent responses can prevent them from obtaining help or assistance. Limited participation restricts the possibility for the exchange of diverse ideas, thus inhibiting the liveliness and richness possible in classroom contexts. When silent, bridges to friendship and understanding are less likely to be made. When students attempt to overcome feelings of isolation by "fitting in," there is the danger that they may feel it necessary to devalue aspects of their home and community cultures, causing them to sever important emotional support. Tracking can be the most significant barrier to problems of isolation encountered by many Type II students. Teachers, who are perceived by students to be caring, considerate, and open, often create classroom environments that foster the free exchange of ideas. Classes that are structured to encourage and promote student-to-student interaction also facilitate students' ability to connect with their peers. Thus, students are more likely to feel valued personally. Programs that offer personal and tutorial support helping this process.

Type III students' worlds make border crossings difficult. Common to this type are students who adapt in some circumstances but not in others. For example, they may do well in one or two classes and poorly in the rest. These students form isolated groups choosing to stay in lower track classes to be with friends. Students' primary concern is their inability to understand the subject content being taught, which causes frustration and worry. At times, pedagogical styles are unsuited to meet student needs. The students' comprehension difficulties are heightened by course content which they find boring, teaching styles that do not take advantage of their strengths, and low expectations which stem from the belief that they are incapable of or unwilling to do well. Some students adapt alternative means to cope with frustrations, such as copying work, creating disruptions in class, or withdrawing from others. Students say teachers who are sensitive and empathetic to problems they encounter in mastering subject matter material influence their feelings about school and their ability to achieve academically. Teacher encouragement and personalized attention are significant. Schools should have supplemental resources to assist students with content mastery, such as peer and adult tutoring programs. Type III students are aware of the implications of failing grades and say they worry about their uncertain future. They say they want to graduate. They seem to have internalized to some extent cultural messages that stress the importance of education for obtaining access to future opportunities.

Type IV students' worlds resist crossing borders. Low achieving students are typical of this type, although high achieving students who do not connect with peers or family also exhibit Type IV patterns. They are at-risk for dropping out of high school prior to graduation due to low grades and lack of course credits. Most Type IV students have given up and blame themselves. Some students alternate between self-blame and criticism of the dominant cultural ideology that anyone can make it, and a system generally unresponsive to their needs. Many students still cling to the hope that they will graduate and often develop elaborate and unrealistic rationales to protect themselves from feelings of hopelessness. They appear to be paralyzed and feel impotent to take action. Their continued failure serves as a reminder that they are incapable of achieving within school-defined parameters of success. These students report that they receive little help or assistance with regard to course selection and/or career possibilities. They describe difficulties with at least one or two teachers. From their perspectives, they are singled out and picked on for reasons of ethnicity, gender, behavior, values and beliefs, and/or personal attributes (Phelan et al. 1991).

Parental emphasis on academic achievement is accompanied by parents' ability to assist their children in matters pertaining to school, such as assistance on homework assignments, communication with teachers and school officials, filing college applications, etc. Parents' financial, cultural, and social capital impacts the quality of help parents give their children. If counselors do not identify students in need, these students are left to face difficult issues on their own. Students across the four types speak of the pressure they experience from peers to participate in behaviors that worry adults. Extracurricular school programs that involve students in activities with their friends are instrumental in providing opportunities for positive peer interaction. Teachers should encourage students to work in groups, fostering discussions in which students talk and listen to each other, and encouraging students to help and assist each other on class assignments. Students must learn to respond to discrimination from peers without anger.

Concerted efforts to impact overall school climate are needed. Schools could have formal structures for resolving conflicts between students and teachers, as well as among students. All these problems have the potential to negatively impact students' ability to engage productively and optimally in school and learning.

Effects of Transition Programs

Smith (1997) found that among a national sample of public school students, those who had full transition programs available to them in their middle school were less likely to drop out of high school and performed better in high school (as measured by student grades) than did students who had either a partial program or none at all. These effects persisted (and for the case of retention, become larger) after family, demographic, student, and other middle school characteristics were taken into account. The positive effects of high school transition programs work for students only when the school provides complete support. Smith says that although it is comforting that transition programs do appear to help, there is clearly greater good to be gained by reducing the contextual problem initially by reducing the numbers of students for which school staff must be responsible. That result is supported by the positive effects on retention noted by the presence of a supportive school-learning environment. School achievement is adversely affected when school programs are not strongly connected with a well-articulated curriculum, two-way communication, and guidance and administrative provisions for smooth transitions (Smith 1997).

Specific Research on Student Transition

In a national study conducted by Queen in 1999, the researcher and author of this text examined the responses of more than 5000 ninth-grade students throughout the United States after the first quarter of school. Table 4 lists the questions and extreme responses that students gave to each question.

Responses of unsure or no opinion were scores in the middle. For example, in question #1, students were asked how they felt about their school. Keeping in mind that their responses are after nine weeks in the ninth grade, 29 percent liked their school and 18 percent disliked the school. And 47 percent of the students had no opinion or were unsure.

Most of the students felt better about the new setting after arriving at the high school prior to the feelings they had before going to the high school. Of importance is the fact that while there were similar or small gains or losses, the problem is the large percentage of students that responded negatively. We cannot afford to have 20 percent of our students having difficulty adjusting to school, or having difficulty making new friends. Interesting that these data compare closely with the near 20 percent of students we lose in schools. We as educators must find ways to lower these numbers.

Lindsay (1998) presents a detailed description of the transition program at Worthington Kilborne High School in Worthington, Ohio. The program focuses on the transition from middle school to high school. The foundation of this program is that all students can learn and the success of students is based on their feelings of comfort and acceptance in their new school. The process starts in October of the year before the students are to begin high school.

The first step is the formation of a transition team. The team members include administrative and counseling staff from both sending and receiving schools, as well as a member of central office responsible for curriculum. It is the job of the team to develop a parent packet which includes the following: a list of meetings and deadlines for writing samples, student profiles, registration, health

Table 4. National Research on Student Transitions From Middle School to High School

How do you feel about this school?

	National
Like	29%
Dislike	18%

How do you feel about the teachers in this school?

	National
Like	24%
Dislike	11%

How do you feel about the way teachers are teaching?

	National
Like	27%
Dislike	12%

How do you feel about the students in this school?

	National
Like	29%
Dislike	9%

How do you feel about the students in your classes?

	National
Like	32%
Dislike	12%

How many friends do you have at this school compared to your last school?

	National
Less	10%
More	71%

Continued on next page

Table 4. *(continued)*

Was fitting in and being accepted a problem for you before coming to this school?

	National
No	82%
Yes	18%

Was fitting in and being accepted a problem for you after coming to this school?

	National
No	81%
Yes	19%

Was getting lost and being late for class a problem for you before coming to this school?

	National
No	84%
Yes	16%

Was getting lost and being late for class a problem for you after coming to this school?

	National
No	79%
Yes	21%

Were older students a problem for you before coming to this school?

	National
No	88%
Yes	12%

Were older students a problem for you after coming to this school?

	National
No	90%
Yes	10%

Table 4. *(continued)*

Was violence and feeling safe at school a problem for you before coming to this school?

	National
No	82%
Yes	18%

Was violence and feeling safe at school a problem for you after coming to this school?

	National
No	86%
Yes	14%

Were drugs and alcohol problems for you before coming to this school?

	National
No	90%
Yes	10%

Were drugs and alcohol problems for you after coming to this school?

	National
No	81%
Yes	19%

Was making new friends easy for you before coming to this school?

	National
No	20%
Yes	80%

Was making new friends easy for you after coming to this school?

	National
No	17%
Yes	83%

Continued on next page

Table 4. *(continued)*

Was keeping old friends easy for you before coming to this school?

	National
No	25%
Yes	75%

Was keeping old friends easy for you after coming to this school?

	National
No	31%
Yes	69%

Was schoolwork easy for you before coming to this school?

	National
No	38%
Yes	62%

Was schoolwork easy for you after coming to this school?

	National
No	46%
Yes	54%

Was school adjustment easy for you before coming to this school?

	National
No	22%
Yes	78%

Was school adjustment easy for you after coming to this school?

	National
No	19%
Yes	81%

records and summer reading lists. A student handbook is also included which contains general information about the school, graduation requirements, rules and regulations, information about the staff, and information from central office.

The team then plans four different dates for meeting opportunities with the principal of the receiving school for parents to attend. At these meetings parents are given the opportunity to meet the principal and voice their questions and concerns and are given a brief orientation to high school procedures and expectations Parents and future students are also given an opportunity to tour the school and see sample schedules. Parents are also asked to complete a series of surveys about their children detailing their expectations and views.

In March the team meets again and reviews the survey information. They then begin to assign classes based on survey information and test scores. In May there is a visitation day for students where they meet the principal again and are given the opportunity to shadow a junior for a day. The incoming freshman get the high school experience while they are still in middle school and the junior gets to play a big brother/sister role.

The school then has a first day of school for freshmen only. The students are introduced to the staff and are then led to homeroom by two senior leader students. Banners welcoming the students are hung throughout the school to make the students feel more like the school is excited about them being there. In the afternoon there is a picnic for all of the staff and students. Throughout the day students are videotaped and a music video is produced and shown at a parent meeting/orientation in the evening.

The results of this program are fewer schedule changes, less first-day absences, and fewer lost students. The first week goes smoothly and parents are surveyed in September about the transition program; this results in high acclaim for this program. Students reported that they believed that the school really cares about them.

In an attempt to describe factors associated with academic success and coping strategies of low-income, urban, minority adolescents making the transition from the eighth to ninth grade, Newman et. al. (2000) assumes that success in high school is directly related to success in college, and that since low-income urban students have a low graduation rate from college it is important to learn how these students cope with the transition to high school. In this qualitative study, the researcher addressed four major questions:

1. What are the relevant microsystems that affect adolescents' motivation and academic performance in the transition from eighth to ninth grade?

2. What are the key elements of those systems that either help sustain or detract from academic motivation and performance?

3. What factors differentiate students who are performing well in ninth grade from those who are having academic difficulties?

4. What strategies do students use to cope with the new and competing demands across settings that accompany the transition to high school?

Newman's research acknowledges the findings of Eccles, Lord and Buchanan in 1996 as well as that of Simmons and Blythe in 1987 which states that "theoretical models that attempt to account for students' adaptations to high school typically do not consider concurrent changes in the students' relationships with their peers, family, and neighborhood during the transition to ninth grade." With this in mind it is also noted that previous research has found the negative outcomes of the transition to high school to include the following: "(a) poorer attendance (Barone, Aguirre-Deandreis, and Trickett 1991; Felner, Primavera, and Cauce 1981; Moyer and Motta 1982; Weldy 1990); (b) decline in GPA (Barone et al. 1991; Blyth, Simmons, and Carlton-Ford 1983; Felner, Primavera, and Cauce 1981); (c) Discipline problems associated with experienceing change to a new school building, moving from self-contained to departmentalized classes, or encountering a different educational philosophy (Moyer and Motta 1982; Weldy 1990) and (d) decreased participation in extracurricular activities (Blythe et al. 1983)."

It is also noted that students who have success gaining acceptance socially in a new school environment experienced smoother transition than those who do not (Schmidt 1993; Kulka, Kahle, and Klingel 1982). A student's feelings of belongingness was also associated with success in school (Felner, Ginter, & Primavera 1982; Goodenow 1993). In short, there are many factors that contribute to either the success or failure of students in transition, not only the factors mentioned above but developmental factors as well.

The *Young Scholars Program* (YSP) involved 29 students, 12 of which had completed the eighth grade and 17 of which had completed the ninth grade. YSP is a program sponsored by Ohio State University and is an early intervention program. Members of their community, teachers or parents nominate students at the end of their sixth-grade year to attend this program. Students must be from a low-income, minority family in Ohio underrepresented in the college population. Admittance is based on the nomination as well as academic performance, potential for academic success, leadership, and other talents or abilities.

The students involved in this study felt that teachers were not as helpful as they may have been in middle school and do not seem to monitor students' work as closely. This led many students to conclude that teachers do not care about them. This resulted in decreased motivation and attendance. These students also felt that the challenges of transition could be broken into four basic categories: relationships with teachers, academic difficulties, adjusting to the school environment, and peer or social pressure. The researchers concluded that if intervention programs are to be set into place and are to be successful, students should be involved as informed experts about the challenges to be faced.

Students also indicated the family as a strong source of support. Efforts to support more successful transitions to high school need to incorporate ways of informing family members about the challenges and demands of the high school identifying strategies to assist with children's academic success. With peer relationships, students felt that the challenge was allocating the right amount of energy and time to their interactions.

As with much of the research, these researchers concluded that transition to high school was a major stressor in the lives of students. This stress combined with those associated with maturation and growth combines to create more stress. The students stated that teachers really matter. More ways of enhancing students-teacher relationships must be found. The findings of the study also confirm that the family plays a key role in supporting academic achievement in school. It was found in order for student success, schools must be sure that every student has at least one adult who is committed to his or her academic success.

Alspaugh explored the nature of the achievement loss associated with school to school transitions from elementary school to middle school and to high school. A statistically significant achievement loss was found with the transition from elementary school to middle school at the sixth-grade level as compared to a K-8 program. Both K-8 and middle school students experienced achievement loss in the transition to ninth grade, however the middle school students experienced a greater loss than the K-8 students. The high school dropout rates were also higher for middle school students than for the K-8 students.

This study cites the following changes associated with the transition to high school:

1. Elementary school goals tend to be task oriented while middle schools focus on performance.

2. Student-teacher relationships change from elementary school to middle school.

3. The change from small-group and individual instruction to whole class instruction in middle school.

4. Researchers have found declines in student self-perception and self-esteem associated with the transition from elementary to the intermediate level.

In 1995 Alspaugh and Hatting found that there was achievement loss in the transition from elementary to middle school, but that achievement scores tend to recover the year following the transition. A statistical significance was found between the dropout rates in the K-8 school and the dropout rates in the two groups from the middle schools. There were two transitions for the middle school groups and only one transition for the K-8 group (Seidman 1994). Students who make two transitions have more difficulty and higher dropout rates that those having less. (See Apendix A for more details about this research.)

As the number of school-to-school transitions within a school district increases, there is an associated increase in the high school dropout rate and socioeconomic status (SES) is a primary factor in high school dropout rates. The following factors have also been determined to be contributing factors: family background, personal problems, and school related problems Relationships between teachers and students, student participation in extracurricular activities and smaller school size are all factors which contribute to lower dropout rates and lower absence rates. (Please see Appendix A for more details about the research.)

Wood and several of his colleagues discovered in 1993 that transition from school-to-school increased the probability that students would drop out. The purpose of the researchers was to explore the relationship of three district organization variables and high school dropout rates while considering the effects of SES. The three variables that were studied were (1) the number of school-to-school transitions, (2) the grade of the last transition to high school, and (3) the K-12 enrollment per attendance center. The sample for the study came from 447 school districts in Missouri. Districts with fewer school-to-school transitions saw the dropout rate decrease substantially. The highest dropout rates occurred when the last transition was at the tenth grade level and most of the students were about sixteen years old. The following beliefs were confirmed: (1) as the number of school-to-school transitions increase, so does the dropout rate; (2) school size is a significant factor in high school dropout rates; (3) SES is a primary factor associated with dropout rates; (4) as school size increases the negative correlation between the percent of students on free or reduced lunch and educational outcomes increases in magnitude.

Steps and Ideas to Improve Academic Achievement Through a Transition Program

In implementing a transition program to improve student achievement, some educators suggest a two step approach. The first step is establishing a set of criteria for identifying the critical transition points in the school continuum, and a process to involve students, teachers, counselors, administrators, and parents. Examples of problems that occur in transitional times are: (a) expectations and standards at each level of schooling are not clearly communicated and understood by the lower level sending school; (b) standards that are defined are quantitative rather than qualitative; (c) far too little communication and collaboration has occurred between and among classroom teachers, curriculum supervisors, and counselors at the various levels of schooling, especially in the area of curriculum content; (d) social promotion from one level to another has caused the need for remedial instruction at each succeeding level; (e) schools at higher levels seldom communicate or feed back data to the lower level sending schools concerning achievement of students at the higher level; (f) enrollments in academic subjects have declined in the high school preparation; (g) overall evaluation of schools is too often done by input measures rather than by student outcomes; (h) students' scores in college-qualifying tests have been declining steadily; (i) college admission standards are not always clearly communicated and selection procedures not clearly understood; (j) some colleges are compromising admissions standards while other colleges are raising admission standards in response to national reform reports; (k) open admission policies in community colleges have not encouraged students to take college preparatory programs; (l) college entrance requirements have had influence on high school curriculum; and (m) a widespread concern exists over the misuse, misunderstanding, and misinterpretation of aptitude and achievement.

The second step for educators to improve transitions and student achievement is for responsibilities at all levels to be clearly defined and assigned to the professional staff. These responsibilities should be contained in the respective job descriptions with clear line accountability. For example, the responsibilities of the counselor at the receiving school should be: (a) to communicate to the sending schools the academic study skills needed for student success as defined by the faculty at the receiving school; (b) to communicate to the sending schools the social, survival and thriving skills needed at the receiving school; (c) to identify and implement procedures for placing students effectively; (d) to identify students who need remediation, acceleration, or enrichment; (e) to use appropriate assessment procedures to evaluate student progress, learning needs, strengths and/or gaps and deficiencies; and (f) to communicate to the sending schools progress, strengths, gaps, and deficiencies of students sent as identified by the faculty of the receiving school. A transition counselor should be appointed to coordinate all transition related programs at the building level.

Another approach is that schools should establish models and guidelines that build on four key components: communication, cooperation, consensus, and commitment. The following elements should be included in the four-step formula: (a) participation by appropriate, empowered people; (b) clear and specific statement of goals, reasonable and reachable, and worthy of the time and effort to be expended; (c) an open agenda, concise and structured, with nothing hidden or pre-determined; (d) convenient meeting times which do not infringe on participants' other duties and responsibilities; (e) incentives in the form of released time, recognition, amenities, limited compensation, and professional rewards; and (f) principles of good group process and decision making.

Perhaps the most important factor in improving transition and student achievement, is to provide students with learning experiences that are logical, continuous and sequential. Often we complain that teachers at the previous level have not prepared our new students. Subject area specialists from all levels in the district should: (a) determine what students should know and be able to do at each level of schooling; (b) spell out specific instructional objectives to be met at each level; (c) agree on content to be mastered and instructional materials to be used; (d) design assessment models to measure the level of skill development and content mastery; and (e) set standards for achievement to use as a basis for remediation, promotion, retention, and acceleration. Teachers must focus on processes as well as product at all grade levels; students can find ease of transition as well as continuity of learning more effective.

One of the most effective ways to narrow the gap between the student's native competence and performance is to know where to intervene appropriately in the process. High expectations should be set for students and communicated to them directly. These expectations and standards should be the result of careful, realistic, consideration for the developmental needs of students at each level, recognizing that the intellectual and social maturation of students of the same age may differ significantly. For example, from grade eight to nine students will: (a) have adequate organizational skills for both short and long term assignments; (b) demonstrate basic study skills such as note-taking, reviewing, and test preparation; (c) consistently completely homework; (d) be able to use memory as a learning tool; (e) be able to budget time; and (f) be able to pay attention in class. Clarifying expectations and standards for students are important early steps in strengthening transitions. (Weldy 1997)

Educators have studied the success of four types of transition reforms. One of these was group advisory periods. Schools attempted to offer early adolescents high-quality instruction from subject-matter experts by departmentalizing programs in which students receive instruction from a different teacher for each academic subject. However, when students change teachers every period, they may feel that there is no one teacher who really knows them, cares about them, or is available to help them with problems. To remedy this, schools have established homeroom or group advisory periods. Many of the activities that occur during these periods are mechanical tasks, such as taking attendance or distributing notices, rather than social and academic support activities that use teachers' talents as advisors and that help students feel someone is looking out for their interests and needs.

Principals in schools with well-implemented **group advisory programs** report that they have stronger overall guidance services and lower expected dropout rates. While principals' estimates of the strength of their guidance services and of future dropout rates are informative, they are imperfectly related to objective measures of guidance-program effectiveness and to actual dropout rates.

Another approach is the **interdisciplinary team** that provides to eliminate the isolation of teachers by providing a working group of colleagues in which to conduct activities, to discuss relevant issues, and to solve mutual problems. Instruction will be more effective in schools that use interdisciplinary teaming because of the increased integration and coordination across subjects, and because teachers on a team who share the same group of students will be able to respond more quickly, personally, and consistently to the needs of individuals. When interdisciplinary teams have formal leaders, teams spend more of their common time engaged in team activities and produce greater benefits for their school.

Remedial instruction in the form of **extra coaching** or additional time to learn is another practice. The most common remedial activities are pullout programs in reading or English, after- or before-school coaching classes, summer school, and pullout programs in math. The practice of providing students who need additional help with an extra subject period during the school day seems especially promising. Other remediation activities may be attended poorly. Pullout classes tend to increase labeling and stigmatizing of students. As for easing transition, an extensive articulation program may be most beneficial (MacIver and Epstein 1991).

Mizelle (1999) stressed the importance of parent involvement to improve student achievement in the transition process. When parents are involved in their child's high school experiences, students have higher achievement, are better adjusted, and are less likely to drop out of school. Parental involvement in the transition process can be encouraged through a variety of activities. Parents can be invited to participate in a conference (preferably at the middle school) with their child and the high school counselor to discuss course work and schedules, to visit the high school with their child in the spring or in the fall, to spend the day at the high school in order to help them understand what their child's life will be like, and to help design and facilitate some of the articulation activities for students.

Without a doubt, quality transition programs can have a positive impact on the overall academic achievement of students. At the high school, it is imperative to have a variety of support programs that address the social and academic problems of all types of youth. While these programs should involve collaboration of all school level staff, administrators at all levels, and parents, research shows that the most important figure in the transition process is the classroom teacher. Teachers should realize the potential they have to positively or negatively influence each student.

4

Examining Exemplar Programs Throughout the United States

The Carnegie Corporatoin Council on Adolescent Development (1996) published a comprehensive report on the needs of the young adolescent, *Great Transitions Preparing Adolescents for a New Century*. The document states that the institutions with the greatest impact on adolescents are family and school, followed by youth organizations, health care organizations and the media. The report further states that increasingly businesses, churches and community organizations are becoming interested in meeting the needs of the adolescent. One area of need for this age student is the need for support transitioning from middle school to high school. Richard Riley cites this need in his *Annual Back To School Address*, "Times of Transition" (2000). Mr. Riley discusses the reformation of the American high school and states that, "Establishing a strong focus on creating an effective transition between middle and high school should be high on our collective agenda as part of this reform" (2000, 6). He further suggests that summer academies, schools-within-a-school programs and freshmen academies, are possible solutions to the issues of transition from middle school to high school.

The adolescent student leaving middle school and entering high school faces a myriad of physical, social, emotional and intellectual issues, all of which can impact academic performance in ninth grade. Programs exist throughout the United States that target the various needs of students making this transition. Julia Smith (1997) conducted a study examining the effects of eighth-grade transition programs on high school experiences. She compared students coming from schools with no transition programs, partial programs and full programs. Full programs are defined as those programs that address the needs of students, parents and staff. Partial programs are defined as those programs that address the needs of one or two of these constituencies. Smith found that full programs provide the most positive effects for students because they include parents and teachers in the transition process. These are the two entities cited in the Carnegie Report as being extremely influential in the lives of these young peoples.

Schools across the United States are experimenting with various kinds of transition programs. Some programs focus directly on the academic issues relating to high school transition, while other programs focus on various areas of student development, such as their social and emotional health. Some programs also address the needs of parents who are facing the challenges of raising an adolescent entering high school. Still other programs support teachers in their efforts to successfully instruct the adolescent learner. Schools with transition programs in place are finding success whether targeting just students or whether they include parents and teachers.

Counseling Centered Programs

Many middle school and high school counseling departments recognize the role they can play in supporting freshman during their first year in high school. DaGiau (1997) has outlined the components of a successful counseling program for middle school students preparing to enter high school. Designed in several parts, it begins in middle school and continues into high school. During *Part One: Orientation*, middle school and high school counselors work with students in selecting appropriate courses for the following year. All selections are subject to parent approval. Students then visit the high school where they tour the school, meet the ninth-grade teachers and receive an overview of high school policy and procedure.

Part Two: Large Group Guidance Sessions takes place during the freshman year. This part is further divided into four sessions. Session one is an orientation session that allows freshmen students to become acquainted with school policies and the requirements for advancement to tenth grade. Counselors meet with students at the end of the first grading period to reinforce what was discussed in the first session. This meeting comprises session two. During session three, counselors begin to advise students on the courses available during tenth grade. The final session allows counselors the opportunity to review issues of promotion and to survey the students about their concerns. Large group sessions operate concurrently with small group counseling sessions. This portion of the program is divided into five sessions designed to cover the topics of personal identity, personal beliefs, decision-making, and goal setting. A fifth session provides closure for the students. In addition to these small group sessions, students benefit from having mentors. Selected upperclassmen serve as role models and mentors for freshman, and assist freshman as needed. The peer-mentoring component of the program is *Part Four* of the overall program.

The final part of the program is geared toward providing support for parents. Parents are invited to participate in an orientation program in the spring prior to their children entering ninth grade. Once their children enter the ninth grade, support continues via parent meetings throughout the year. Parents are also invited to attend special programs relating to topics pertinent to adolescent development.

Other counseling programs also exist to ease the transition into high school. One counseling program that has met with success is "A Write Way," a structured narrative writing intervention program designed to foster resiliency during transition (Lewis 1999). The program is a structure-relationship model that is designed to enhance the student-adult relationship in the school and to create an environment that clearly communicates high expectations for students. The program is built on the premise that writing has inherent powers to help students chart their way though the stressful transitions that are part of life. Students who take control of their own narratives may be able to change the direction of their story and thus their lives.

A study was conducted using two of the six structured narrative lessons that compose "A Write Way." The study was conducted in a rural high school in California whose population is largely minority. The lessons were offered to students in a ninth-grade math class. The lessons orient students to graduation requirements, help students develop school-related narratives, assess their role in school, assist in problem solving and help students set goals for themselves (Lewis 1999).

Lesson One was a highly structured lesson that conveyed the requirements for high school graduation. Because the lessons were conducted in a math class, the students were provided with a mathematical formula for the graduation requirements. Additionally, several writing prompts evolved from the question, "Do you plan to graduate from high school?" Working through this lesson helped the students understand the expectations of high school. *Lesson Two* provided students with the opportunity to analyze their personal experiences with school. The students were asked to respond to the prompt, "Write a make-believe letter to your worst teacher." Working through this assignment allowed students to articulate some of their fears and difficulties with school. It also provides counselors with the opportunity to work with teachers, assisting them in creating caring, learning communities.

The goal of "A Write Way" is to allow teachers to convey high standards to students and to be the caring adults that students need in order to meet those standards. Through the use of structured narrative writing, teachers and counselors can help students understand the expectations of high school, offer them support, and ultimately help them re-author the stories of their lives and change the outcome of their school experience.

Some counseling programs are designed to allow teachers to assume limited counseling responsibilities with students. Robert Myrick designed the Teacher Advisor Program (TAP) so that high school students would have the opportunity to interact with a caring adult on a regular basis. Small groups of 15 to 25 students meet with a teacher to discuss such topics as getting acquainted, self-esteem, time management, computing grade-point averages, and school policies. Teachers participate in training sessions with trained counselors in order to become comfortable building the guidance lessons for their group. This program continues throughout the four years of high school, so that all students have the support of a caring adult and a peer group throughout their high school career.

Another program designed to allow more involvement of teachers in counseling activities is in place in the Sarasota County School System in Florida (DaGiau 1997). The Teacher Advisor Program provides time for counselors to meet and work with classroom teachers. During these working sessions, teachers develop supplemental material to address the social and developmental needs of the adolescent. The ultimate goal of this program is to promote success in school by providing more personal attention for students.

Salem High School in Eugene, Oregon, has successfully developed a student advocate program. Each teacher at the 700-student high school is placed with a freshman student to help the student in the transition process. The average student-to-teacher ratio ranges between three and five freshman students. Teachers help students to develop a career track and a Personal Learning Plan that takes into account where the student is academically and socially, with student goals denoting specific areas of strength and areas in need of improvement. Students designed these goals with limited teacher input (Vonvillas 2000).

One student at Salem spoke candidly about his own experience with the transition processes. He stated that he entered Salem High School from a very small parochial middle school. Fearful of the high school experience, his fears were realized when his English instructor asked him during the first week of high school to read a passage of poetry aloud. Uncomfortable at reading aloud, he stumbled and stuttered, utterly embarrassed. After class, the teacher met with the student and discussed his fears. The two of them decided this issue was one that the student would like to improve upon, and they decided to meet with the students' advocate to discuss an action plan. Together, the student, the English teacher, and the student advocate developed an action plan. By the end of the semester, the student was self-assured and confident with his reading skills (Vonvillas 2000).

Orientation Programs

Other programs for students' transitioning into ninth grade have experienced success. These programs strive to make students aware of the demands of high school life and offer support during the transition process. Over 200 high schools in the United States make use of the *Link Crew Program*. This program links freshman with specially trained senior peer mentors. Each senior is assigned a group of approximately 12 freshmen to mentor during the critical first year. The students get together for social events that aim to welcome the freshman students and to project a sense of belongingness onto the newcomers. They also meet for assemblies on more serious topics such as school problems, study habits, and the impact of freshman grades on the overall GPA.

Hebron High School in Carrollton, Texas, has designed *Hawk Camp* for its incoming freshman students. Sophomores and juniors run the day-long camp. It is designed to combine social activities with small group discussions. The upperclassmen share their freshman year experiences, easing newcomers' anxieties. The freshmen write goal-setting letters to themselves, a task that helps them focus on long-range planning.

Writing a letter to yourself is the culminating activity of the four day *Gifts Unlimited Teens Seminar* (GUTS). This particular program is not sponsored by a school, but rather by a nonprofit agency. This program, which is geared to rising freshman, focuses on identity, values, team building and decision making. Teens share in discussions that help break down stereotypes and stress the similarities in people. At the end of the four days, the participants write a letter to themselves listing the insights gained over the four days. Ideally students will take these lessons with them as they enter their new high school (Holmstrom 2000).

The Peer Group Connection, a component of the Princeton Peer Leadership program, trains seniors to act as mentors to high school freshman (Fazio and Ural 1995). The program is in place in high schools in the Northeast including districts in New York, New Jersey and Philadelphia. The seniors selected for the program, along with their faculty advisors, undergo training in human relations and facilitation skills. Through this program freshman are involved in school activities, interacting with students outside their usual circle of friends. The success of the program is measured by improved grades, attendance, and behavior on the part of the freshman. Since its inception, the program has grown to include a *Peer Counseling Corps*. This specially trained group of seniors works individually with freshman students who are experiencing more difficulty with the high school transition, and are not performing well academically. The seniors provide counseling and academic support to the ninth grade students.

One example of how important a successful orientation can be is that of *The Freshman Getaway*. Held at Franklin Pierce High School in Tacoma, Washington, in August, this 12-hour event combines the traditional high school orientation with food, fun, entertainment, and bonding. Beginning in the previous spring, counselors from the high school visit the local middle school to introduce the concept of entering high school. Through the eighth grade language arts classes, they introduce the course catalogue, definitions of high school terms (credit, semester, career path, etc.) and graduation requirements, and begin to help eighth graders build their ninth-grade course schedule.

This process takes three to five days and culminates in an evening parent meeting that includes the principal, department chairs, coaches, activity advisers, and counseling staff members. At this meeting, parents are introduced to the Freshman Getaway concept. The getaway is then held one week before school starts. Students form groups of 10 to 15 students, which include a staff member and a junior or senior helper. The groups conduct an icebreaker activity and are assigned a special task for the day, which helps to promote team building. Later tours are given and a presentation is conducted which addresses topics of student interest. Last year's topics included: what to do in unpredictable situations, getting involved, what teachers expect from students, and what students can expect from teachers, and understanding and acceptance. Since the program's inception, Franklin Pierce High School student questionnaires indicate that students feel more at ease with their surroundings and with themselves and other classmates, compared to those who have not participated in the transition program. Over the three-year period since the program's beginning, a decrease has occurred in the high school dropout rate. Although no concrete evidence indicates that the transition program is the reason for the drop, school educators and students have stated that they feel it definitely is a component to student success (Hewins 1995).

Programs for Special Student Populations

Some programs are designed to meet the academic needs of specific groups of students. Minority students from families of low socio-economic status, who are at risk of not completing high school or attending college, are often the subjects of special programs. One such program is the previously discussed *Young Scholars Program* (YSP) in effect in several urban Ohio school districts (Lohman, Newman, Myers, and Smith 2000). This program targets promising sixth grade students and follows them into high school. Students who are accepted into the program are promised admission into Ohio State University and a loan free financial aid package upon successful completion of the program. Students and their parents must agree to participate in year-round YSP activities, complete college preparatory courses, maintain a 3.0 grade-point average and attend summer sessions at Ohio State. As part of the program, students were monitored during their freshman year. Their input was solicited so that program directors could gain a better insight into the difficulties associated with transitions.

Systemic Change

At the Air Academy High School in Colorado Springs, Colorado, all freshman students take part in a *Learning Resource Lab* for one block during their first semester. The LRL is a combination study hall, homeroom, and advisory group. Activities to assist the transition to high school are built into the LRL. The activities include a study hall with adult tutoring, a conflict resolution workshop, career exploration, technology exploration, a study skills and note-taking seminar, an introduction to various clubs and organizations, and a review of the student handbook/policy manual. Instructional Paraprofessionals advise and teach the students in the LRL.

This program was instituted after parents and students complained that the adjustment to high school was difficult because students were not managing their time nor did not have the study skills needed for a rigorous high school schedule. A survey of students involved indicated that students appreciated receiving the tutoring and assistance. In the three years since its implementation, administrators have documented that freshman have fewer failing grades, fewer discipline referrals to the assistant principals, fewer suspensions, fewer absences, and a more positive attitude toward school (Pierson 1998).

The faculty and staff at Kettering High School in Detroit, Michigan, recognized the correlation of success in ninth grade and completion of high school (Reinhard 1997). In an effort to increase success in this grade level, the school community has instituted several initiatives. The school employs an attendance counselor and social worker required to monitor attendance and provide discussion sessions. Freshman students receive additional counseling sessions, take a basic course of study and attend most classes in a separate wing of the building. In addition, targeted rising freshman attend a five-week summer session geared to providing a preview of high school life. Kettering High School has found this program to be successful. A noticeable decline has occurred in the number of ninth graders who drop out of high school, while an increase has occurred in the academic achievement of freshman students.

The growing awareness of the need to support freshmen during the transition process has prompted some school districts to analyze the grade configurations in their systems. The Cache County School District in Utah has taken on this task and initiated changes in its grade configuration. Two stand-alone Freshman Centers have been established in the Cache County School District. The centers, North Cache Freshman Center and South Cache Freshman Center, are designed to meet the unique academic, physical, social and emotional challenges facing freshman students (Zsiray 1996.) Freshmen are housed in a separate building where the transition from the middle school to high school can be done gradually. This allows the students to get to know the classmates without dealing with upperclassmen. The staff counsels students on the importance of doing well in the freshman year, and explains how freshman grades impact the GPA in the senior year. Yet, the centers also set expectations that they believe to be appropriate for ninth graders.

The expectations are higher than those expected in middle schools, but they are not as initially rigorous as those that are in a traditional 9-12 high school. Students are provided with the opportunity to receive additional support as needed with their academic work.

The centers maintain close contact with the high school that the students attend in tenth grade. The centers have the same school colors, mascot and student activity cards as those in the high schools. Freshmen students participate in all extra-curricular activities held at the high schools. The students are viewed as the freshman class of the high school. Reaction to the program thus far has been quite favorable. While the North Cache Freshman Center and South Cache Freshman Center are housed in separate buildings, the concept of a freshmen center can be adapted to a school-within-a-school model. The basic premise is to allow freshmen the opportunity to have a gradual introduction into the rigors of high schools. While Freshman Centers or Academies can be most effective for transition, I must offer one warning. Too much isolation of the Center or Academy can actually create the need for another transition—going to tenth grade. I encourage more integration of the freshmen, with sophomores, juniors, and seniors.

5

Developing an Effective Transitional Plan for the Local School System

Change can be scary. One of the most difficult and frightening changes occurs when a middle school student enters high school. Now more than ever, the phrase "growing up is hard to do" rings true. Many educators compare this transition with a baby leaving the safe, comfortable, nurturing womb and entering the "real grown-up" world. The transition becomes even more frightening when the student feels alone. As previously discussed, many schools have established programs designed to smooth the way for students. Schools are for students, and we know that the more comfortable a child is with the learning environment, the more likely the child will achieve, both socially and academically. Keys to making these transition programs work include meeting the student at the student's level, personalization of high school, good student-teacher relations and student-student relations, and community/family support (Hewins 1995).

When speaking with eighth graders, the most common topic they want to discuss is the transition to high school. Even by the beginning of their eighth-grade year, most students are already thinking about the change that will take place the following year. Many students experience worry, fear, and full-blown anxiety when thinking about high school. Couple this transition with the other changes that occur during this critical life stage, such as the physical changes children experience, and a major life event leaves students describing the transition as "the most terrifying thing I've ever done" and "so bad I don't even want to talk about it" (Davis 1998).

Such trepidation has led educators to devise unique ways to address this issue. Most transition programs address students' fear first. For example, orientation has taken on new forms and consists of more than just times to sign up for classes and meet new teachers. Often the orientation programs have various components that span the time of several days to weeks in length. Students are invited to attend cookouts with their new teachers and other freshmen. Upperclassmen are often invited to speak about their own experiences with transition and to offer answers to questions new students voice.

Lounsbury (1999) found that there are several key components to success for transition programs. First, the orientation must be student-centered and appeal to student needs. In the past, orientation has taken on an almost lecture-type atmosphere. Students have indicated that this type of format is boring and dull. Students did not retain information that was shared, resulting in students who felt lost and uncertain about the faculty's expectations of them, as well as their own expectations of themselves, other students, and teachers. Students gain more help from programs that are interactive and fun.

Another component of an effective transition program is the concept of a personal adult advocate. This could be a teacher or administrator who is available to the freshman student and offers help with questions or academic problems. This type of personalization is achieved when teachers and students have the time and the desire to develop relationships. Teachers often teach best when they know their students well. The trust that develops from such a relationship cannot be minimized, especially for a new student who feels uncertain.

Considerable staff development is needed for achieving a personalization program. Dedication, monitoring, and support of both student and teacher are essential. Sometimes teachers experience difficulty transitioning from instructor and assessor to the role of guide, facilitator, and listener. Administrators need to be aware of this and help to tailor programs to these needs (Creswell and Rasmussen 1997).

Equally important in the transition process is the student-to-student relationship. The upperclassman's role in helping the freshman student to feel comfortable has been over-looked in the past. Yet, peer relationships are most crucial during these years. Several schools have devised a "buddy system" in which a junior or senior is assigned to one or two freshman students over the school year. The buddy's role is to act as mentor and confidant to the new student. These types of programs have proved to offer a good support system. However, they need constant supervision by staff, and it is crucial that the program be well-structured to ensure that time spent with the freshman students does not exceed limits and that all students involved are comfortable with the arrangement (Lounsbury 1999).

The middle school transition programs over the last 15 years have shown that the administrative/organizational changes are often the easiest part of the job. The far more demanding phase of the process is bringing about changes in people, their attitudes, and their assumptions. Such programs must evolve from soul-searching and trials. As educators we know what works for one school's population may not work for another school's population. To change school climate and the attitude that freshmen possess regarding the transition, all stakeholders must be involved in the process. People make a school. The quality of relationships and the openness of teachers and administrators to reach out and connect with students have a crucial impact on the high school experience. When community volunteers become involved the process is even more beneficial (Mizelle 1997). Central to fostering academic success and social development are schools in which all students feel a sense of belonging and are welcomed by staff and upperclassman. With support, dedication, and patience, middle school transition can provide students with an opportunity for growth, adventure, and lasting social relationships. All of these parts are integral to a solid learning foundation.

This is the model of a program that I feel will assist students to avoid many of the pitfalls they face during the transition period.

IMPACT
Introducing Model Power for Achievement in Constructed Transitions

Phase One

By March:

> Set up classroom visits for middle school students by transition team members, administrators, and selected students to distribute information on programs offered at high school.

> Develop a brochure/student handbook to be distributed at visitation that contains school information such as a list of the academic demands of high school, graduation requirements, health records forms, a list of important test dates, information on different programs, clubs academies, and extra-curricular activities.

> Assign rising Junior Mentors to groups of 4 to 6 rising freshmen and give junior students credit as part of a service learning project.

> Develop dates and program for "Meet the Faculty" nights to be held in May and August and include rewards for participation —tickets to game etc.

> Develop a survey for current ninth graders to determine needs of incoming freshman based on their own experience as well as to assess the effectiveness of current programs.

> Create a shadowing opportunity for incoming freshman. There are many varieties.

> Develop heterogenous ability levels in cohorts or school within a school on the ninth grade level—team concept or academies.

> Involve current eighth grade administrators and faculty in vertical teaming and in high school preparation. Developing a Vertical Teaming Committee is a good first step.

Implement a freshman camp in August before school starts including an orientation session for students and parents. This will create a feeling of welcome and a desire to have the freshman here, strongly encourage involvement

Components of Proposed Summer Program

- Introduction—expectations, requirements, study skills, facts on dropouts and success, planner information, grading scale, handbook review, clubs, activities, sports

- Strategies for success—Academic, Individual, and Social

- Academic—relationships with teachers, behavior, assignments, studying, and enrichment activities . . . establish an Advisor/Advisee program

- Individual—hard work, determination, focus, priorities, self-discipline, effective use of time

- Social—positive influences, teacher and parent encouragement, extra-curricular activity

- Tour of Building/Campus—walk through of schedule, introduction of teams, administrators and counselors.

- Team Meeting—Review of specific expectations, availability of team for tutoring, explanation of special programs.

- Conclude with a picnic lunch at the end of the day with faculty, student government representatives, athletes, club representatives, and junior mentors.

Major Objectives of Phase One

- The student/parent will be (TS/PWB) comfortable and feel invited in the building

- TS/PWB comfortable and familiar with the staff.

- TS/PWB comfortable and familiar with their individual schedules

- TS/PWB familiar with the expectations and guidelines of the high school.

- To eliminate to the greatest extent possible apprehensions and transitional roadblocks to student success

Phase Two/Phase Three

- Create a "Modified Block Schedule" to accommodate the special needs of ninth grade students.

- Freshmen attend one full day of school before other students begin school.

- Implement a freshman seminar course that incorporates "high school culture" content as well as any additional transitional concerns discovered.

- At-risk students are assigned remedial course in area of need (teacher uses creative instructional strategies . . . including diagnostic/prescriptive approaches of teaching and assessing student progress.)

Sample Modified Block Fall Schedule

A Day

- 1. Science

- 3. Remedial Class

- 5. Freshman Seminar

- 7. Elective

B Day

- 2. Science

- 4. Remedial Class

- 6. Freshman Seminar
- 8. Health/PE

Sample Modified Block Spring Schedule

A Day

- 1. English 9
- 3. Algebra I
- 5. ELP
- 7. Elective

B Day

- 2. English
- 4. Algebra I
- 6. ELP
- 8. Health/PE

Phase Four
Assessment and Evaluation

Traditional and authentic test results will be analyzed in addition to a detailed case study of the freshmen class. Interviews and survey data from parents, teachers and students will be included. An evaluated report will be given to the principal/superintendent by June 30.

Phase Five
Modified Summer Camp
for Incoming Freshman

Results from the tests results and recommendations from the report will assist the committee in making appropriate adjustments with the next freshmen class.

6

Defining the Problem

Students moving from the middle school to high school anticipate having more choices. Along with this anticipation comes concerns about teasing by older students, making lower grades, getting lost in a larger unfamiliar school, and having more difficult work. For many students, this change can become an unpleasant experience quickly. Many students view themselves more negatively and experience an increased need for friendships. By the end of tenth grade, 6 percent of America's students drop out of school (Owings and Peng 1992). Many argue the dropout rate to be 25 percent or higher. This critical transition time becomes another stressful experience for some students who are already a high risk for violent behavior.

Violence is defined as immediate or chronic situations that result in injury to the psychological, social, or physical well being of individuals or groups. Interpersonal violence is further categorized as behavior by persons against persons that threatens, attempts, or completes intentional affliction of physical or psychological harm (American Psychological Association 1993). School officials must be familiar with these definitions and be prepared to recognize and react to all elements of violence in their schools.

The intensity of violence involving children has escalated dramatically over the last two decades. Homicide is the most common form of death for young African-American females, as well as for young males. Children are becoming involved in violence at younger ages. Schools, being part of the social fabric of society, are not immune to these facts. For this reason, schools must accept major responsibility in combating this societal problem.

In many instances, the school environment is conducive to aggressive behavior among students. The composition of school environments that inadvertently promotes violent behavior among students include: large numbers of students in a limited space, heavy-handed and inflexible use of rules in the classroom, teacher hostility and lack of rapport with the students, and inconsistencies in the limits of tolerance for student behavior. Considering these facts, the age and size of many of our high school structures may contribute to the problem of violence. A large portion of school buildings built in the 1950s and 1960s were designed before school violence was a major focus *at least in middle America* (author's emphasis). In addition, economic considerations have forced many districts to fill high schools with populations of 2,000+ students.

Often when violence does enter the school environment, it usually takes the form of a bully or gang. Gang problems are no longer confined to the inner city and must be understood by school administrators at the national level. The membership in gangs is rising and encompassing a wider range, from 9 to 30 years of age. Ninety percent of gang members are ethnic minorities, and males dominate gang memberships twenty to one over females. The popularity of gangs results in the fact that they meet the developmental needs required of all youth, which include a sense of belonging, a feeling of connection, and self-definition. Given the fact that it is three times more likely that homicide and aggravated assault will be perpetrated by a gang member and that gang violence often occurs from provocation, school administrators must be prepared to combat this epidemic in their buildings. One should note that the overcrowding of school institutions increases the likelihood of this event occuring.

The other most common form of school violence is the presence of bullies. It is believed that 15 percent of children are involved in bully-victim problems and that bullies regularly harass one in ten students. Although the behavior of bullies might be viewed as a childhood problem, the aggressive behavior must be acknowledged and combated by school administrators. The pervasive ethic of aggressive behavior in the school environment detracts from the curriculum. The everyday suffering on the part of the victim can lead to runaways, attendance and academic problems, and even suicide (National School Safety Center 1995).

Societal Costs of School Violence

Schools not only have the responsibility to operate a safe and effective organization but also the responsibility to develop and to promote productive citizenship. The proliferation of minorities involved in gangs results in a direct relationship in the likelihood of being involved in a violent crime. Bullies are also likely to face a lifetime of failures. Aggression and disruptive behavior in schools contributes to poor school achievement and peer relations. Bullies are more likely to be career underachievers, dropouts, to perform below grade level, and to become abusive spouses and parents. Frequently, former bullies perpetuate the cycle by building a new generation of students with similar social interactions (National School Safety Center 1995).

Not to be ignored in this discussion is the potential social effects displayed by victims. Females who are victimized by sexual abuse and assault may display immediate psychological and behavior effects. However, it is not uncommon for psychological consequences to manifest themselves over a number of years and appear once the individual has reached adulthood. Male victims are more likely to withdraw from school activities and develop attendance problems. Sadly, an increase in the chance of suicide, and a greater likelihood of bringing a weapon to school for protection or retribution are also negative reactions. These facts should magnify the need for successful intervention at the school level and reiterate that bullying is not a necessary component of childhood.

School leaders struggle to eliminate these concerns and make students feel more comfortable at the high school level. Many administrators, in their haste, make damaging mistakes. In an effort to reduce anxiety and school violence, many educational leaders across America have demonstrated poor judgement or carried school rules too far. For example, a Harvard University study released in June 2000 showed that children in various U.S. schools had undergone suspensions for bringing a plastic toy ax to school as part of a Halloween costume; for carrying unlit sparklers inside a book bag; and for being in possession of a toenail clipper. In one school district, what looked to most as an innocent eight-year-old in the school cafeteria, willfully, and with malice aforethought, pointed a chicken strip at a second-grade classmate and said, "Bang." The chicken strip was not loaded, but the student ran into a "zero tolerance" policy in place at his school. He was suspended for a day (Cosh 2001).

Not to make light of the mistakes of administrators who act before thinking, serious problems exist in America's schools when one looks at the increase in violent acts by students. Although information is sketchy and sometimes contradictory, data suggest that incidents of aggression and violence are increasing at an alarming rate. In 1994, school officials reported 3 million violence-related acts. According to some reports, 1 in every 10 students is a victim to some act of aggression (Furlong, Morrison, and Dear 1994).

These violent acts can be correlated to several common circumstances and behavioral and environmental characteristics. Numerous examples in recent news reports illustrate how aggressive, antisocial children tend to look at themselves and their surroundings. Many students in middle and high schools are often self-centered and very inconsiderate of others. The standards they have learned for managing their behavior are different from those of others. Many students have not been taught to or are reluctant to assume responsibility for their actions (Walker, Sprague, and Hill 1999). Before middle school and high school, these social characteristics are for the most part not destructive and can even be amusing. By the time students are ready to transition to high school, these characteristics can be highly destructive and anything but humerous.

Fortunately, properly trained school officials have the potential to identify and intervene in the development of potentially violent students. The greatest predictor of violent behavior is a previous history. Therefore, students who display early aggressive behavior must be identified at the earliest opportunity provided and effective systemic intervention must be implemented in order to avoid escalation.

Societal Factors Resulting in Violent Students and Victims

Many other factors are also involved in the development of violent students. Family characteristics, the breakdown of the traditional processes and relationships, and harsh and continual physical punishment by parents contribute to the problem. In addition, ethnic minorities that have limited pathways to participate in mainstream American culture have the potential to resort to violence. For these reasons, school officials must be aware of the social situations of all students and be able to identify factors that may lead to violent behavior. Windows of opportunity in the social development of these individuals are available to implement effective treatments. Transition points are conducive to quality intervention maximizing effectiveness.

Although perpetrators are victims of their social development, school administrators must be able to identify victims and potential victims of violent behavior in order to offer support and interventions. Vulnerable populations within the school include girls and young women, frequently prone to sexual violence and assault. Gay and lesbian youths are also a vulnerable population. Although there are psychological gains to identifying their sexual orientation to the student body, the result of this decision could put their physical and mental health in jeopardy. Children and adolescents with physical and mental disabilities are also disproportionately vulnerable to school violence (American Psychological Association 1993).

Our society is producing thousands of young adolescents who come from surroundings in which they are exposed to numerous risk factors that can be detrimental over time (Loeber and Farrington 1998). Strong and clearly established links exist between these factors, the behavior and reactions resulting from their exposure; the short-term harmful effects on the developing child that flow from this exposure; and the destructive, long-term outcomes that often complete this developmental process. Ultimately this proves to be very costly to the individual, to caregivers, friends, and associates; and to society at-large (Vance, Fernandez, and Biber, 1998). Other correlates of school violence include substance abuse, victimization, marital discord/spouse abuse in the home, depression, exposure to violence in the mass media, and extreme poverty.

As more and more children experience an array of risk factors, increasing numbers have selected an unfortunate path, which too often ends in school failure and dropout, adult crime, delinquency, and sometimes violence. Many of these problems begin in the middle school and during the transition to high school. Older students in the high school create less discipline problems as they mature. Discipline problems also decline at the upper grades due to the fact that many students at risk for violence drop out before completing their high school experience—a problem that will reverse if states require the dropout age to increase without supportive programs.

There are many risk factors unrelated to the school, which may lead to school violence. Five specific risk factors have been identified through longitudinal research for both youth violence and delinquency. Middle school and high school students who are involved in multiple risk conditions—(a) the mother and/or the father has been arrested; (b) the child has been a client of child protection; (c) one or more family transitions has occurred (death, divorce, trauma, family upheaval); (d) the youth has received special education services; and/or (e) the youth has a history of early and/or severe antisocial behavior- are at severe risk for adoption of a delinquent lifestyle (Hayne and Alexander 1997).

Violent crime and victimization have become part of life for many youth in the United States. While adolescent deaths from other causes declined during the past 20 years, death rates have increased dramatically due to interpersonal violence. The second leading cause of death among adolescents is now firearm-related. For African-American adolescent males, firearm-related incidents have become the leading cause of death. Furthermore, adolescents increasingly are becoming the victims of crime, are experiencing greater fear of crime, and witnessing more crime than their counterparts 20 years ago (Sells and Blum, 1996).

Attitudes among some youth support violence. In a study of New York City high school students surveyed in the 1991-1992 school year, more than 50 percent suggested walking away as an effective way to avoid a fight, but 20 percent endorsed carrying a weapon and 21 percent endorsed threatening as ways to avoid fights.

Media coverage of violence in schools suggests a dramatic increase in the 1990s. Today violence no longer concerns only inner city school districts. It has now become a problem for school districts nationwide. It is unclear whether a real increase occurred in violence, or if an apparent upsurge occurred due to increased reporting by school districts. The reluctance of school administrators to report violent incidents increases the difficulty of understanding the problem. Teachers' unions and other professional organizations have prompted much of the reporting of violent attacks by students on teachers and between students (Hayne and Alexander 1997).

Though violent attacks on students and teachers attract media attention, the majority of aggression is less extreme, consisting of bullying, verbal/physical threats, fistfights, shoving, and other simple assaults. Since childhood aggression is usually a precursor of later adjustment problems in middle and high schools, schools represent the most logical setting in which to counteract the reinforcement and practice of these undesirable behaviors.

Some claim violence in schools reflects a violent society and some research supports that much of what occurs in school begins outside the school. Violent behavior in general is linked to the experience of violence at home, to victimization, and to witnessing violent acts.

School Efforts in the Prevention of School Violence

Most of the work that has been conducted around violence in schools is slanted and non-experiential, and conducted by experts in sociology, law enforcement and criminal justice rather than by school administrators. More research is now including school officials and provides a more complete picture of the causes and effects of violence in schools in the near future, but this work is not being accomplished soon enough.

Prevention is always a better solution than reaction; administrators and teachers must find ways to identify those students who may become potentially violent. The primary problem is that until now educators have been in the reactive mode. Law enforcement and school administrators, working hand-in-hand, may be able to provide opportunities for such prevention. Administrators must now listen more closely to students to determine their needs and be attune to cues students may be providing that can prevent violence if acted upon (Wood and Hoffman 1999).

During the transition between middle and high schools, students are faced with the issue of acceptance. Some of these students are already challenged with special needs. Recent school reform has focused on inclusion of students with disabilities into the regular classroom. It is predicated on a philosophy of acceptance of all students, but the current focus on diversity does not mean that all students with disabilities are being accepted with enthusiasm back into the regular classroom. Students who are verbally defiant, abusive, or physically aggressive, pose a special problem when placed in the least restrictive environment.

The United States has a violent history as a country, and many experts argue that America, by nature, possesses a violent culture. We should examine the school environment in order to reflect upon new directions and how systemic changes can be designed for improvement. Obviously the first place to start is with student transition between grade eight and nine.

The unfortunate exception to a general downturn in violent crime in the general population involves an upsurge in violence among youth. Violence often results when minor infractions escalate. As school violence increasingly has become widespread, schools have become the location of many violence prevention efforts, few of which have been evaluated adequately. Violence in middle schools and high schools is getting worse, not better as often reported. Educators must not overlook this issue. An important focus must be placed on decreasing violence in young adults during their middle and high school experience, specifically during the transition between the two levels. Limited bullying and scare tactics are growing without being reported.

Aggressive behavior perceived as a right of childhood can be identified and remedied with thoughtful planning. Fortunately, administrators and community officials have sufficient research to identify and combat the problem.

Gibson (2001) examined the perceptions of the School Resource Officer (SR0) regarding the selection criteria and specific job expectations for a law enforcement officer working within the secondary school setting. The SRO is a vital link toward the success of the communication process between students and school leaders. However, she found no consistent standards or procedures used by SROs across the nation and no significant plans for standardization.

Contrary to common belief violence in the United States has reached epidemic proportions. Especially troubling is the increase in violence among youth with a predictable overflow into the public schools. Violence in and around schools has become more common and more serious. [National Center for the Analysis of Violent Crime (NCAVC) 2000].

Although national research has shown lower school rates of violence reported since 1993, the increase for deadly school violence is on the rise. The increasing level of serious school violence frightens teachers and students and appalls administrators. High rates of violence have caused concerns addressed by many alternatives, a key one among them being SROs in public schools. School Resource Officers are one option that communities have adopted in addressing violence. The SRO program was developed to help school officials cope with the growing incidence of school violence and to make the school environment safe and conducive to enriched learning. Since its inception of the School Resource Officer program, the concept of the SRO has spread throughout the United States. The placement of police officers in city schools has had a positive effect on school violence and disciplinary infractions.

The placement of police officers in high schools and middle schools was a proactive measure designed to prevent school fights; theft; drugs and alcohol use; the possession and use of weapons, and other school related problems. The need for SROs in the schools is vital to keep schools safe.

Gibson (2001) discovered that principals view the role of the SRO as primarily law enforcement oriented. She believes that role conflict inhibits the job performance of School Resource Officers. The researcher also believes that until there is a job description for SROs that clearly defines their roles and responsibilities in the school in which they work, there will continue to be conflict between the expectations of the principal and the SRO. In addition, she further stated that survey research focusing on the selection, job expectation, roles, and responsibilities of the SRO will be useful in designing a written job description for SROs in the nation.

Public secondary schools recently have become quite interested in police/school relationships. The research is sketchy, quite possibly because schools do not want to publicly admit that violence is becoming a serious problem. One may ask, Then why do we have police stationed in our schools? Researchers suggest that deterring crime may be one of several reasons school administrators want police in schools. Also, a positive relationship with an adult who is available to provide support when needed is one of the most critical factors in preventing student violence (Dwyer 1998).

School Resource Officers who are housed in schools have rarely been studied. Their role in this unique environment is often seen as a paradox, as they support students on one hand and enforce the law on the other. SROs are more than law enforcement officers on campus; they fulfill three roles within their school communities. The major role of the peace officer who prevents violence by keeping the peace, serve as teachers who instruct students in their area of expertise; and act as counselors who serve as conduits to community resources.

The overall goal of the SRO is to provide a safe school environment conducive to learning. This goal is accomplished by reducing the prevalence of weapons, drugs, and gang related activities; monitoring students' movements; maintaining a secure school environment; providing support to school administrators, teachers, and staff; providing counseling services to students; dealing proactively with trespassers; and, being highly mobile, visible, and flexible (Johnson 1999). The SROs' main purpose is to develop a rapport with students so that students trust them enough to either inform them about other classmates planning violent incidences or turn to the SRO for help when they find themselves in trouble (Mulqueen 1999).

Both school and law enforcement personnel desire input to determine the role of the SRO. Funding and evaluative considerations may complicate the expectations and role orientation of the SRO program. Funding for the SRO position is often a joint endeavor of both city police departments and local school districts. This can create competing priorities. The SRO is evaluated on different criteria in differing programs across the country.

The SROs' duties consist of serving as a positive role model for students, teaching law enforcement classes, acting as a counselor, and handling criminal investigations on the school campus. Primarily, they are considered educators and role models that provide safety, counseling, crime prevention, and awareness programs to students but most educators feel safer, we really wish we could return to the days of violent-free behavior.

7

Reducing Teacher, Student, and Parent Fears

The school violence that occurred in California and Pennsylvania has focused the nation's attention on the issue of youth violence and school safety. Principals at middle schools and senior high schools, more than any other position in our educational system, are under pressure to address the issue of school safety, and as school leaders they cannot shy away from the fact that violence has unfortunately become a major focus in the schoolhouse (Mizelle 1997). School districts around the country have implemented a number of policies to address school safety. Zero tolerance policies for weapons and drugs are the most widely known. Intelligently developed, clearly communicated, and fairly administered, these policies can meet parental and social expectations and protect students' and teachers' physical well-being. Zero tolerance policies alone, however, are not the answer (Mac Mullen 1996). Safe schools are more than schools that are free from violent incidents. Principals should ensure a positive school climate, in which each student is engaged and inspired to achieve to the highest academic level. Schools, and in particular high schools, must personalize the school experience for each student. Positive school climates must ensure that every student is well known by at least one adult in the school (Mc Iver 1990).

Transition to High School

The beginning of high school remains a very critical time for students. Educators know that the time of school transition can be problematic for students as they face a new, more anonymous environment and greater social and academic demands. For ninth graders, the pressure of making a school transition can be amplified by the developmental struggles they are facing as adolescents, leading to a greater chance for negative outcomes. In her review, Legters (2000) reports that many ninth graders have a difficult time adjusting to the demands of high school, which result in lower grades, more disciplinary problems, higher failure rates, and feelings of not "fitting in" to the high school community.

Violence is more prevalent when students: perceive their classes as not teaching them what they want to learn; do not consider their grades important; do not plan to go to college; and feel they have no control over their lives. Students who make poor grades are more likely to be discipline problems and to commit violent acts. In fact, students with poor grades are three times more likely than all students to threaten someone with a gun or knife and four times more likely to threaten a teacher (Louis Harris and Associates 1998). There are connections that schools, families, and communities must make to address these attitudes.

Over the past 10 years, threats and injuries to students and the theft and vandalism of student property remain at steady but high levels (National Education Goals Panel 1993). Children themselves recognize the problem. Nearly one-fourth (23 percent) of America's public school students say they have been victims of an act of violence in or around school. However, an almost identical group (22 percent) are "somewhat worried" or " very worried" about being hurt by someone else when they are in or around school. Serious discipline problems are more common than violence in the schools; however, twelve percent of teachers surveyed nationwide reported that student misbehavior interfered to a considerable extent with their teaching. There are concrete actions that schools can take to make their schools safer for all students. (Gallup 2001).

Peer Support Program

The belief continues to exist that peers are important sources of influence and support for each other. Various programs in high school such as peer counseling, peer leadership, peer support, and peer mediation can provide incoming students assistance in dealing with their daily stresses and anxieties. Students making the transition into the high school need to know that they will have a peer support program in place. The goal of such a program is to put them in touch with older peers and to provide a forum in which to discuss and listen to various relevant issues. The program includes: making friendships; understanding relationships with parents and the changes in the construction of the nuclear family; understanding sexuality and the social attitudes toward sex in an era of AIDS; making decisions about drugs and alcohol use; and pursuing academic achievements; and exploring career choices. Teenagers are more open to peers than to adults when it comes to accepting information about how they come across as individuals, about reasonable alternatives in solving different problems, and about opinions regarding possible ramifications of their behavior.

Ten years ago Horn and West (1992) suggested policies and procedures to reduce students' and parents' fears. Below is a partial list:

1. School personnel must firmly enforce the zero-tolerance policies toward weapons, alcohol, and other illegal drugs, as well as ban tobacco use on campus. Local laws must be enforced, as well as school policies. Alternative suspensions should be provided where possible and appropriate.

2. The necessary data to be gathered and shared must be identified by officials.

3. Officials must establish agreement and systems for communication, which should include what is to be said and who is to be contacted, as well as other systematic procedures.

4. School personnel should set forth positive expectations, clear rules, and the penalties for violating rules for students.

5. Administrators should design student contracts for specified improvement in behavior and consequences for when students violate the contracts' mutually agreed-upon actions.

6. Schools should insist that all students put outerwear (jackets, coats, sweaters, and similar out clothing that could conceal weapons) in their lockers during school hours.

7. Schools should require all students wear shirts tucked in to help prevent hidden weapons being brought into classrooms.

8. Schools should develop and enforce dress codes that ban gang-related and gang-style clothing and consider establishing a pre-scribed standard or style of dress or instituting a policy of school uniforms.

9. School officials should develop random searches of classrooms for weapons and other contraband. They should consider requir-ing that backpacks, duffle, and tote bags are mesh or transpar-ent so students, teachers, and others can see what is inside.

10. School officials must make it clear that gang or gang-related behavior in school will immediately involve severe sanctions. They should work with police gang experts to track potential troublemakers.

11. Schools should establish a policy of positive identification. Administrators, teachers, staff, and students should wear photo ID badges; visitors must wear appropriate IDs that are issued at a central location. Police officers, as well as school staff, should be authorized to question and detain trespassers without IDs.

12. Schools should deny students the permission to leave school for lunch and other non-school related business.

13. Schools should ban beepers, headphones, and cellular phones on school property.

14. Schools should ensure that pay phones with no-charge access to emergency services are strategically placed in and around the building.

15. Schools should ensure that, as graffiti appears, it is removed as soon as possible.

Has much really changed in the last decade?

Parent Involvement

The importance of parent involvement can hardly be overestimated in their young adolescent's transition from middle school to high school. When parents are involved in their students' transition to high school, they tend to stay involved in their children's school experience. When parents are involved in their children's high school experiences, students have higher achievement, are socially adjusted, and are less likely to drop out of school.

As previously discussed, parent involvement in the transition process to high school can be encouraged through a variety of activities. In planning activities for parents, high school teachers and administrators will want to remember that parents of students who are already are excellent resources for other parents and may also help encourage new parents to be more involved in school activities. At the middle school level, teacher and administrators can inform parents about transition activities and encourage them to participate. Mizelle (1997) emphasizes the fact they can work to keep parents involved in their child's education and school activities during the middle school years so that they are comfortable "coming to school" and confident that their involvement makes a difference in their child's academic success.

Training

Schools and school systems seldom offer staff any formal training in collaborating with parents on how to make schools safer. Teacher training programs can include: general information on the benefits of and barriers to parental involvement; information awareness of different family backgrounds and lifestyles; techniques for improving two-way communication between home and school; information on ways to involve parents in helping their children learn in school and outside; and ways that schools can help meet families' social, educational, and social service needs. Allstate Insurance (2001) recommends the following strategies for staff development on parent involvement:

Schools and school systems seldom offer staff any formal training in collaborating with parents on how to make schools safer.

1. School and police staffs should be trained to work together to handle emergencies and crises. Select parents and mature students could be asked to participate in the training.

2. Staff and students should be trained in how to effectively take reports from students concerning suspicious activities or concerns and in how to ensure proper follow up to the reports.

3. Teachers should be trained on how to break up fights with minimal risk and on how to handle the situation if a student brings a weapon, especially a firearm, to school.

4. Staff and police officers should be trained in anger management skills and in how to teach them to students. Anger management concepts can be infused into all academic areas.

5. All school staff, as well as any law enforcement officers who work with youth, need to know the warning signs of troubled adolescents and need to know the community resources to refer them to in order to receive the necessary help.

6. Schools should hold parent meetings to discuss indicators of risk. Community agencies can develop training and parenting skill classes to help parents communicate the dangers of violence and drug abuse to their children and sharpen their own skills in dealing with their children's problems. Police and school staff should be included in these sessions.

7. Law enforcement needs to talk to parents about: the importance of safety storing and securing all guns (and storing and locking ammunition separately); the dangers that such weapons present, even if secured; and the potential parental liability.

8. Students need to know which school personnel or student peers can be approached if they are angry, depressed, or need help working through a problem.

9. Teens can be a wonderful resource in designing and running programs such as mediation, mentoring, peer assistance, school crime watch, and graffiti removal programs.

10. Students can be a resource in maintaining a good learning environment. A teen court can easily try minor offenses or determine punishment for those who have pleaded guilty to violations of either school rules or community laws.

11. Anonymous reporting systems should be developed to let students share crime-related information in ways that do not expose them to retaliation.

12. A suggestion box should be available for students to offer ideas about reducing violence, drugs, or other crimes at school. Public feedback should be provided for credibility.

13. A "red flag" system should be set up to ensure that reports about students who exhibit warning signs of violence or self-destructive behavior—whether from peers, faculty, police, or parents—receive immediate attention.

14. School districts should develop—with social services, youth workers, and others—a comprehensive truancy prevention effort that engages police, as well as school staff, in the importance of enforcing school attendance laws.

15. School personnel should conduct periodic safety audits of the school's physical environment and should examine the potential trouble spots for unsupervised access, for vandalism, for students who might be outside of reasonable supervision, and for congested areas that might create tension among the students.

16. School personnel need to work with community mental health staff, substance abuse counselors, the faith community, and other practitioners to make sure that students, faculty, and staff know about a variety of resources that can help troubled students.

17. School administrators must provide adequate security at all school events that take place after school hours.

18. School districts can invite juvenile probation personnel to staff an office full-time or regularly visit in the schools.

19. Schools can assist local mentoring organizations in establishing relationships with at-risk students.

20. Schools should establish emergency intervention teams that include students, teachers, and counselors. The teams need to be trained in emergency management, crisis and grief counseling, and related skills. Drills and mock emergencies should be conducted on a regularly basis.

21. School personnel must build and maintain an inclusive educational environment. Students, who feel bias or prejudice because of race, gender, religion, or sexual preference, might take their anger out on the institutions they view as responsible.

22. School districts must ensure that security and safety are fully considered in setting, designing, and building additional facilities.

23. Community agencies and school districts should develop joint-use programming. The Recreation and Parks Department or another community agency can use school buildings for after-school programs; athletic leagues for youth can provide activities.

24. School personnel should establish student assistance programs that help students find the necessary resources to deal with such problems as substance abuse, violence or anger management.

Perhaps the best thing that we can do today is talk to our children as parents and our students as students, and of even greater importance, we must listen. We know that with the most deadly acts in our schools' history, every shooter told someone what he was going to do (U.S. Secret Service 2001).

8

Responsibility and Civility

Throughout history, schools have been assigned the task of developing students into responsible, civil citizens, and citizenship has been the basis upon which curriculum has rested. Even in the times of the founders of our democracy it was stressed that education was to be focused on devotion to the public good. Then and now the welfare of our nation has rested upon an educated citizenry and the premise that public schools could best be used to teach the values and knowledge necessary for a functional society to exist (Berman 1997).

It is the basic purpose of a universal literacy to assimilate productive, contributing citizens who are prepared to handle local, national, and world issues. In a society that functions under democratic principles, it is important for individuals to make rational decisions and understand the consequences of their behavior, while being accountable for their choices and actions. (Queen 2002).

Academic subjects are important and essential, but they do not prepare young people to be functioning citizens. Unless academic subjects are presented in conjunction with some form of civil education, little is to be gained by students to prepare them for life in society. Therefore, the importance of addressing the teaching of responsibility and civility in our schools is paramount, as it has been over time. If we are to produce students who will be well-adjusted, contributing members of society, teachers must guide them to be responsible and civil through the provision of experiences that make the concepts relevant and understood. Students will then be equipped with the knowledge necessary to understand their role in society.

Constant conflict in our schools can bring about the destruction of a school environment. Therefore, the teaching of responsibility and civility is very relevant to educators because the demonstration of these behaviors in students provides a positive, non-destructive school climate. An environment is determined by the way the people in the environment deal with conflict situations. Consequently, when students are taught to behave responsibly and to exhibit polite, civil behaviors to peers and adults, they are more likely to possess positive attitudes that transcend each aspect of the school setting. This will bring about the development of a nurturing, productive environment. Teachers are able to effectively provide instruction, allowing students to be engaged in active, productive activities. Focusing on the development of appropriate behaviors by stressing responsibility and civility enables students to be better equipped to demonstrate appropriate social interactions. Because they have been taught strategies that enable them to control their own behavior, discipline problems are alleviated before they transpire. Therefore, the school climate is a positive, quiet one that promotes learning and allows learning to occur.

Focusing on the teaching of techniques that promote civil behaviors exposes students to problem-solving strategies that can be implemented in dealing with conflict situations. The students are consistently provided with opportunities to put these techniques into practice. Opportunities might include allowing student input in rule-making and development of consequences, or activities that facilitate student participation in events that promote peer interactions, such as cooperative learning activities and group projects. In providing these types of opportunities for students, the responsible, civil behaviors become habitual, integral parts of the students' daily lives.

Students who develop and use behaviors that are responsible and civil grow into responsible, civil adults. They develop and maintain positive self-concepts that enable them, as adults, to deal effectively with social and professional interactions. These adults are more equipped to become contributing, successful members of society. Students must evolve into community citizens that are well-adjusted, hard working, and successful (Berman 1998).

Positive Effects of Teaching Responsibility and Civility

Evidence shows that although students today are no more irresponsible or disrespectful than those of a decade ago, there is a growing number of students turning to violent measures in dealing with conflict situations at school (Stover 1999). This can be attributed to any number of societal factors, including an increase in single-parent homes, increased incidences of violence demonstrated on television, and lack of parental supervision due to the increase of families in which both parents work outside the home.

It is believed by educators that providing students with strategies that develop the behaviors of responsibility and civility will enable them to resort to peaceful solutions. Also, the teaching of strategies that improve cooperative learning activities will result in higher levels of academic achievement and more cohesive group interactions.

It is imperative that schools focus on developing the character of students. In doing so the students are held to high expectations. These students are expected to be responsible enough to take ownership of their own behavior and learning situations. During instructional periods these students will be on task, focused, and more able to retain presented information. These same students will be more adept at handling peer interactions during cooperative or interactive learning activities because they have learned skills that improve socialization abilities such as respect, patience, teamwork, and communication. With high expectations and an organized curriculum, these students will be more successful in the academic setting, thus developing positive self-esteems. The students will feel good and be more willing to cooperate. This attitude of cooperativeness provides a climate of hard work and cohesiveness, where students get along with each other, and teachers are actually teaching without constant disruptions. Teachers in these settings maintain lower stress levels and feel a higher sense of accomplishment.

Each individual student within the school setting must maintain a sense of responsibility and civility because without these values, the students are less able to function effectively in group situations. Students who know how to follow rules or standards function better in the classroom and perform better academically. The structure provided in these settings offers students a secure, nurturing environment that provides comfort and stability, allowing students to grow and thrive in both social and academic areas (Queen 2002).

In a school that has developed students who are responsible and civil, there is a warm, inviting climate. Members of this school community treat each other with respect and are willing and able to demonstrate that they care about others. This environment is one in which optimal learning can and does occur, and student achievement is apparent. Students are taught how to live better lives, and have developed virtues and habits that are a necessary component of a civil society. "A young person cannot spend 12 or 13 years in school and be morally unaffected by the experience" (Ryan 1997). It is the responsibility of educators to ensure that the experiences provided are positive ones that develop and maintain good character. When the focus of schools is to provide positive activities and experiences that make the students feel good about themselves, the effect on the school climate is positive.

Consequences of Excluding Responsibility and Civility Instruction

Because the viewing of television and computer-related activities have become the major leisure time activities for young people today, there is much less time spent participating in civic activities or activities that promote personal interaction with others (Lewis 1998). A lack of personal involvement coupled with the lack of parental support, supervision, and direction is depersonalizing students. With this depersonalization, and a lack of focus on the teaching of values and moral behavior, comes a lack of social skills and a social instability that initiate any number of behavioral disorders, such as disrespect, uncooperativeness, depression, and inattentiveness. Therefore, these students are unable to acquire skills that are needed to demonstrate appropriate social interactions in the school or the community.

Teachers understand that to reach these students they must spend a great amount of time developing and implementing instructional techniques that will make learning experiences for them exciting, relevant, and rewarding. Although strategies used in many classrooms are extremely innovative and engaging many students are not equipped with the skills needed to function appropriately in the school environment. They have spent the majority of their time outside of the school setting engaged in isolated activities or have not been provided with guidance or direction in developing morals and values. Often these students spend so little time interacting with others that they seldom have the opportunity to develop appropriate socialization skills. Therefore, when interacting in the school setting, these students may not see themselves as behaving inappropriately even when it is apparent that they are.

As a result, if educators refuse to accept the responsibility of becoming a change agent in order to provide for the needs of students as they relate to character development, the schools are in great danger. The results of a lack of focus on developing character traits in schools have been evidenced in many schools throughout our nation. Within these schools, there is a lack of vision, no clearly defined mission statement, and a poor overall school climate. Because students' needs are not adequately addressed, students are more apt to handle conflict situations inappropriately, greatly increasing the number of discipline problems within these schools.

Due to the increased number of discipline problems in many classrooms resulting in the lack of focus on the positive character development, teachers are forced to deal with many more classroom disruptions. The time spent addressing discipline problems diminishes classroom instructional time and this most certainly will affect student progress. Students spend less time on-task, causing the levels of learning to decrease. Consequently, student achievement levels are low as are students' self-esteems. When this occurs the result is a poor school climate.

With the constant interruptions and lack of optimal teaching opportunities, teachers and staff lose their enthusiasm. When faced continuously with disrespectful students who care nothing about school classroom rules, morale becomes low, and the ability to effectively handle discipline problems decreases. Teachers in these environmental situations are likely to maintain poor relations with colleagues and superiors. Time spent interacting with other adults is time spent complaining about the many problems that exist due to the lack of appropriate student behavior. These teachers are less likely to compliment peers or notice effective practices being implemented in other classrooms.

Parents in this setting are also negatively affected by the low morale and poor interactions. They are less likely to be actively involved or available to offer assistance in the classrooms or other areas within schools. It is also unlikely that the parents will maintain positive relationships with teachers or other school personnel. Fund-raising activities and school spirit activities will be minimal or non-existent. A void is left that cannot be filled in any other manner other than parental involvement. Without this support it is difficult to achieve positive progress within school environments.

Another important component that is also negatively affected when these issues are not addressed is community involvement. Community members are not likely to work closely with schools maintaining a poor climate or atmosphere because it is difficult to work with students who consistently exhibit irresponsible, uncivil behaviors. The school also portrays a negative light on the surrounding community, making community members distance themselves and withdraw from the school. This leaves another area of void within the schools, further impeding the progress of the schools and the students within them.

These are consequences that educators are faced with when they continue to ignore the need for the inclusion of concepts in the school curriculum that focus on the development of responsibility and civility. Such was the case at Allen Academy, a public school located in the Dayton Public School System (Bernardo and Neal 1997). The school was a magnet school located in the center city that served a culturally diverse population. Three quarters of the 537 students at the school received Aid to Dependent Children, and over half came from single-parent homes. Students in this school were not taught to value responsibility or civility. There was no parent involvement, and the community was not encouraged to take an active role in school affairs.

After experiencing years of low test scores, numerous students suspensions, low teacher attendance, and limited parent involvement, the principal and staff of the school began to investigate the practices of more successful schools. They determined that Allen Academy was lacking a number of components that were necessary to improve the school climate and increase student achievement. These components included the development of a school mission statement, the inclusion of a character development program in the school curriculum, and programs that promoted increased parent and community involvement. Table 5 demonstrates the changes achieved at Allen Academy within only a few years of the inclusion of these practices.

As demonstrated in the example of Allen Academy, when the inclusion of character development programs focus on teaching responsibility and civility many benefits are evident in schools that choose to implement them. When students behave appropriately they feel better about themselves. Teaching and learning can occur and good things happen all day, every day. On the other hand, educators who continue to ignore the need for the inclusion of these concepts will be forced to deal with the many consequences that are not only detrimental to the school environment, but to the success of students.

Table 5. Results of Allen Academy 1989 and 1995

Allen Academy: 1989	Allen Academy: 1995
Ranked twenty-eighth of thirty-three schools in the district	Ranked first in the district
Teacher attendance lowest in district	Teacher attendance highest in district
150 students suspended	Eight students suspended

Strategies for Teaching Responsibility and Civility

In addressing the need for the development of responsibility and civility in students, educators must understand that the social foundations of the school and methods of instruction are the central means for teaching responsibility and civility. The classroom and school must be open, and a nurturing environment must be apparent. Personal relationships should be valued, with caring for others being included as an important aspect of learning situations (Berman 1997). Therefore, the school must be child-centered and include school spirit activities, and service projects in curriculum. In doing so, the school becomes a democratic community where students are allowed to participate in decision-making and feel free to express their opinions in a non-judgmental atmosphere.

In working towards a child-centered atmosphere teachers must provide equitable amounts of attention, support, and encouragement to all students (Lasley 1994). This can be done by consistently using positive statements during instructional activities, placing positive comments on papers and projects returned to students, and by circulating among students' desks and providing reinforcement during independent work activities. In doing so, students are less likely to feel the need to speak out at inappropriate times. There is a high level of classroom monitoring that helps alleviate classroom disruptions and promotes the use of civil behaviors among students.

Within this setting the teacher must provide the students with strategies for appropriate reactions in the event that conflict situations do occur. This can be addressed in rule development activities in which students actively participate. Students assist the teacher in determining classroom rules and consequences that accompany the breaking of those rules. Conflict situations must be dealt with promptly in order to alleviate the assumption of students that the inappropriate behavior is tolerable.

In conjunction with the implementation of these strategies, there needs to be an emphasis placed on cooperative learning activities. Students should be provided a number of opportunities to work and socialize in groups in order to promote a high level of interaction. Implementation of these practices also aids in the development of effective communication skills, higher-level thinking skills, and promotes the use of resources of other students. This emphasis also lessens competitiveness and the need for students to compare themselves against other students.

The classrooms should be organized in such way that they act as role models in conflict situations. Clear guidelines must be set and time must be allowed for students and the teacher to identify behaviors that are disruptive to the class and the learning process. The teacher must also take the time to explain why certain behaviors are unacceptable and allow students to participate in the development of a list of consequences for these behaviors. This provides students with a sense of ownership and makes them responsible for their own behaviors.

To further promote the development of responsible and civil behaviors in students, the classroom instructional techniques should include lessons that enable students to appreciate the importance of civil, responsible behavior (Lasley 1994). Teachers must have available in the classrooms literature that focuses on these concepts and should also include these forms of reading in their teachings. These concepts may also be included in social studies and health lessons. Providing these types of opportunities for students to experience exposure to behaviors that demonstrate responsibility and civility makes the concepts relevant to students, and provides them with strategies for using these concepts in their own daily lives.

Also effective in promoting students responsibility and civility is the emphasis of the importance of rights and responsibilities as part of the students' roles. Whenever possible students should be allowed to resolve conflict situations on their own. In promoting this action students must be asked questions that enable them to demonstrate understanding of what actually transpires in situations of conflict or inappropriate behavioral displays. In doing so, students will begin to develop ways to better handle themselves and their behaviors.

Students must also be provided with opportunities to be responsible, such as with the use of classroom chores or leadership positions. As a result, students will develop an appreciation of the value of intrinsic rewards and their self-concepts will improve. Students will feel better and will be more conscious of how they treat others. With the development of these abilities students will work harder and will be more likely to give their personal best in all situations.

A final component that will further enhance the school environment with the development of responsibility and civility in students is the inclusion of character development programs that promote these concepts. Therefore, these programs must include life lessons that promote problem-solving, the development of social skills, and conflict resolution. The inclusion of peer mediation programs will also be beneficial in that these programs will enhance the abilities of students to behave responsibly, due to the understanding of expectations and their own personal skills (Queen 2002).

Within their classrooms, teachers must demonstrate their care and concern for students. In doing so, students will acknowledge that they are valued as a person, which will enable them to value themselves and their communities, as well. Teachers must take the time to encourage students to think of themselves as dream-makers, peace-makers, and heroes. As a result, they will work harder to achieve their goals, and the goals established for them in the school setting.

Programs and Models Promoting Responsibility and Civility

In working to achieve an environment where students develop positive self-concepts and values, teachers will need to reinforce the development of positive attitudes and feelings by providing students with ways to best handle themselves in conflict situations. A model that is specifically designed to aid in the development of these strategies is the Holton Model for Conflict Management (Holton 1998). This model contains three parts: (1) problem identification, (2) solution identification, and (3) solution implementation. Problem identification entails investigating the situation in order to apprehend adequate information in attempting to make a decision in regards to how the situation might be best handled. Solution identification involves analyzing the situation in order to develop alternatives and solutions for dealing with what has happened.

Solution implementation provides a means for developing a plan of action, and also allows for the determination of ways to best handle the same type of situation in the future. Using a model of this type provides a means for conflict situations to be analyzed and understood, and is likely to alleviate the repetition of these same situations in the future.

Another effective approach to providing strategies to students that will promote positive character development is the Responsible Classroom Management (RCM) Program (See Table 6) (Queen 2002). This program focuses on students taking responsibility for their own behavior. The basic premise is that all students are capable of learning responsibility, with the provision of logical consequences that help students self-direct their own behaviors. Teachers are expected to exhibit responsible behaviors, and this prompts students to make more appropriate and acceptable choices in dealing with difficult situations.

In the RCM program, compliance is based on responsibility, not obedience. Therefore, the appropriate behaviors of students become a natural part of their normal behaviors. This approach provides a healthy, positive way to manage and maintain student behaviors.

Table 6. The Responsible Classroom Management (RCM) Program

Basic Components of the RCM Program:

- Clearly stated instructional objectives

- The inclusion of instructional activities throughout the school year that focus on the teaching of responsibility

- A warm, inviting classroom environment

- High student participation and interactive instruction

- The use of standards and guidelines, rather than rules and consequences

Another approach to the development of positive character traits in students can be found in what is called the Peace Keeping Model (Reardon, 1988). This model is designed to enable students to maintain rationality and control in the midst of hostile circumstances. The steps of this model include the following:

- Step back, take a deep breath

- Share your feelings; listen to others

- Solve the problem; choose options

- Act on the solution; move forward.

In conjunction with the teaching of these steps to remain calm and rational during conflict situations, the teacher should expose the students to procedures that will improve the students' abilities to maintain a positive frame of mind when faced with problems. Procedures might include those outlined in the Peacekeeping Procedures (Reardon 1988). These actions include:

- Using words to solve problems

- Applying communication, interaction, and decision-making skills

- Utilizing a mediator

- Using "I" statements

- Attacking the problem, not the person

- Attacking the problem at hand without dragging in past problems.

Providing students with strategies of this type that enhance their abilities to deal with conflict situations will aid them in being more equipped to seek peaceful solutions. A successful program to further emphasize the importance of the inclusion of character development in the school curriculum that emphasized the teaching of responsibility and civility, a character development program that has been successfully implemented will be discussed. This program is the SAFE Program, developed and implemented in Orange County, Florida (Stover 1999). The program incorporates the following:

- Lessons in anger management, conflict resolution, and interpersonal relationships

- The inclusion of these concepts in the existing Social Studies curriculum

- Emphasis on parental involvement

- Peer mediation programs

With the implementation of these strategies there has been a marked drop in student suspensions, absenteeism, and low student performance. Schools throughout Orange County have shown great improvement in school climate and student achievement.

By maintaining student-centered classrooms where clear expectations are apparent, students' rights and needs are addressed, civility and responsibility are promoted, and a positive school climate is maintained.

School Spirit Activities and Service Projects

In conjunction with the inclusion of character development programs, there needs to be a focus on self-esteem building activities. Activities that will further enhance development in these areas include provisions for school spirit activities and service projects.

The school spirit activities should focus on recognition of individuals and the school membership as a whole for accomplishments and positive interactions. Examples of these activities might include the following:

- School Pep Rallies

- Attendance Awards

- Character Education Parades

- School Spirit Day

Involvement in school spirit activities provides many opportunities for students to observe and practice good behavior. These activities also offer wonderful ways to promote parent and community involvement in schools activities. In doing so, the morale of students, staff, parents, and community members is maintained at a high level, and a positive school climate is achieved.Another important component relates to participation in school-sponsored service projects. In focusing on the implementation of service projects as a component of the school curriculum, educators must agree and make students understand that they can contribute to the welfare of the community and the welfare of the planet by the actions they take. Students must learn that responsible people not only make rational choices and decisions and accept the consequences of their actions, but they care for and respect the rights of others (Lamme et al. 1992). Because responsibility is learned through experiences, students must be given greater responsibility in order to develop into more responsible, socially effective individuals (Berman 1997). Students will grow to understand and value themselves through their appreciation of others. The school environment will then develop into one in which students, staff, parents, and community members will choose to work harder towards the goal of producing students who are able to demonstrate appropriate behavior on a consistent basis, without teacher prompting or token rewards.

Participation in these projects is essential to cultivating responsible, civil behaviors in students because activities of this nature promote the awareness of shared needs, and this facilitates the building of empathy and civility. Through these activities, students learn that part of being responsible is caring for one another. This enables students to learn to respect the rights of others, thereby developing moral reasoning skills and promoting positive and appropriate interactions. Simply providing students with exposure to academic subjects does not enable them to recognize that they are part of a community and that their actions will affect their ability to function well within that community. Schools are social institutions and the educators within these institutions are given the responsibility to provide students with socialization skills that will enable them to function as productive citizens. Teaching responsibility and civility will make this possible.

Participation in service projects further demonstrates for students the importance of deeds in developing personal responsibility towards others. In developing personal responsibility towards others, students become more aware of how their actions and behaviors affect others, and are better equipped to make good decisions regarding their treatment of others by the way they choose to behave. Some examples of school-sponsored service projects include:

- Fund raisers for a special cause

- Collections of food/clothing for needy families

- Visitations at area hospitals/nursing homes

All of these activities combine into a wealth of experiences for students that enable them to evolve into responsible, civil individuals.

Role of the Principal

In working to ensure that students are developing skills that will enable them to behave responsibly and with civility, the principal must play an active role in addressing needs in these areas. One way in which the principal might demonstrate involvement is through emphasis of the school mission statement. Knowledge and understanding of the school mission statement by staff, students, parents, and community members must be pursued. This can be accomplished in allowing parent and staff input in the development of the mission statement. Also, consistent review of the statement at staff meetings, parent meetings, and in school newsletters or publications will provide adequate reinforcement.

The principal must be visible during school activities before, during, and after the school day. The principal must promote a positive attitude about the school activities, demonstrating excitement about the things going on in the school and the community surrounding the school.

Another important area that the principal must actively participate in is school recognition activities. These activities may include:

- Formal recognition assemblies

- Principal's Awards

- Positive comments to students as encountered through-out the school

The principal's participation in these activities provides a positive role model for the staff and students to emulate, and sets a positive tone in the school setting.

A final component that will further provide the principal with assistance in promoting responsible, civil behaviors in the school setting is the implementation of activities that bring the community and school together. These activities might include:

- Participation in activities offered by museums, zoos, art galleries, and cultural centers

- Partnerships with local businesses and merchants

- Partnerships with local colleges and universities

Participation in these types of activities provides students with numerous role models who exhibit good character and responsible behaviors. Students are also given opportunities for more individualized instruction and discussions relating to behavior issues. These activities also offer cultural exposure to students, further enhancing their background knowledge, thereby advancing improvement academically and socially.

Impact on Student Achievement and Behavior

In order for students to reach optimal achievement levels the school environment must be one that is conducive to learning. Students and staff members must demonstrate responsible, civil behaviors that facilitate the development of a positive school climate. Not only will students increase social skills development, they will also be more open to learning opportunities and instructional strategies that will increase academic achievement. These students will feel a sense of responsibility, respect the rights and needs of others, and work diligently to succeed.

A society where there is no sense of responsibility and civility is one where there is no moral code. Every person lives by his or her own moral code, and this brings about a self-centered mentality that breaks down the fibers of our communities.

As educators we must have as our goal the development of students into moral, ethical people who are responsible for their actions.

Students must grow to function in society through their learning and think rationally about the consequences of their behavior, while being held accountable for their actions. (Lamme, Krogh, and Yachmetz 1992). If students in schools are to become successful, contributing members of society, schools must accept their role in ensuring that students are taught the concepts of responsibility and civility.

Removing the Bully Factor from Transitions

Adolescence is a time of tremendous change for students. In fact, adolescence can be accurately described as a time of physiological, academic, and social turbulence. Caught between childhood and adulthood, young people face: a bewildering array of choices; emerging but not yet realized independence; new social and interpersonal relationships; and changes in their school environments. Students face at least four major school changes before they graduate, not including disruptions caused by family dislocations, changes in economic status and family breakup. Students transition from pre-school to kindergarten, from kindergarten to elementary school, from elementary school to middle school, and from middle school to high school. Each transition brings with it: a change in friends and social structure; a change in academic expectations and, teachers; and often, in schools. The transition from middle to high school, however, may be the most traumatic, because it occurs in the period of greatest personal physiological, psychological, and social change. Most young people navigate turbulent adolescence with relative ease and success, while others find themselves buffeted by relentless waves of academic failure, social rejection, and increasingly, school violence.

Recent incidents of extreme forms of school violence, such as shootings and stabbings, have forced school leaders to focus on school safety and researchers to look for the underlying causes of school violence. An array of factors contribute to school violence: ethnicity and social status, the presence and use of drugs and alcohol, perceptions of school safety, and the post-traumatic stress experienced by children as either victims or witnesses of violence. But, as Anderman and Kimweli (1997) note, although "research on violence has focused on the media, the community, and the family as causal agents...*the school largely has been ignored in studies examining violence and bad behavior during adolescence*"[emphasis added] (p. 4). Nevertheless, because a school's culture can contribute to violence, educators have a crucial role in planning the reduction of violence in schools.

Unfortunately with the major focus on serious and deadly violence, educators feel numb to the thousand acts of "low-level" violence that occur in schools each week. Like the proverbial "frog in the kettle," extreme violence gradually anesthetizes administrators' sensitivities to "lesser" forms of violence. Name-calling, shoving, vandalism, insults, school-yard pranks, and other forms of bullying pale in comparison to the wanton shooting of students and teachers. With sensibilities dulled, it is tempting for administrators to dismiss bullying as unpleasant but normal adolescent behavior and to chalk it up as "kids being kids." This is a mistake because bullying may be a catalyst for future delinquency and more extreme acts of school violence for both the bully and the victimized student. A student's environment, rejection by peers, and exposure to aggression, either as perpetrator or victim, is strongly associated with future delinquency and violence, according to a large corpus of research.

When dealing with bullying, it may be useful to view bullying and violence on a continuum of behavior rather than as unrelated behaviors. At the low end of the continuum is bullying, which Espelage, Bosworth, and Simon (2000) define as "a set of behaviors that is 'intentional and causes physical and psychological harm to the recipient.' Bullying includes actions such as name-calling or teasing, social exclusion, and hitting" (p. 327). Similarly, Huesmann (1994) defines aggression, a form of bullying, as: "a behavior that is intended to injure or irritate another person" (p. 330).

Unfortunately, bullying is rampant in our schools. According to studies cited by Espelage et al. (2000): "Seventy-five percent of adolescents reported some form of victimization from a bully during their school years" (p. 327). The National Association of Elementary School Principals reports that, "one in ten students is regularly harassed or attacked by bullies [and] 15 percent of all schoolchildren are involved in bully/victim problems" (p.1). Of growing interest is the increase in bullying by girls. Simmons (2002) identifies what is called relational or social aggression. Girls don't use their fists, but bully with dirty looks, gossip, turned backs, negative gestures, or isolation of their victims. This type of bullying usually begins by third or fourth grade and continues throughout high school.

A school environment that permits bullying to go unchecked is one that may be inviting more extreme violence. Citing Bandura's social learning theory, Espelage et al. (2000) notes that:

> The external environment contributes, in large part, to acquiring and maintaining aggression. Children learn from role models, including adults and peers, to use aggressive means to achieve their goals. [Moreover], the relationship between early aggression [bullying], peer rejection, and exposure to violence...later violence is strong. The author found that students who bully were themselves at an increased risk of being physically abusive and of having a criminal record as adults. (p. 328)

"It is difficult to find any other childhood factor," write Huesmann and Guerra (1997), "that predicts more of the variation in adult aggression than does childhood aggression" (p. 408). Echoing similar findings, Arsenio, Cooperman, & Lover (2000) argue that: "Beginning in the preschool years, childhood aggression is an important predictor of difficulties in social functioning and adjustment" (p. 438). Ladd & Profilet (1996) have found that "Children's use of aggression...consistently emerges as one of the best predictors of later adaptation....aggressive behavioral styles are predictive of peer rejection...and children who display aggressive tendencies...appear to be at greater risk for adjustment problems in early adolescence" (pp. 1008-1009).

Likewise, Stattin & Magnusson (1989) observed that when "compared with low and normally aggressive subjects, the early high aggressive subjects...were involved in more serious crimes [and]...were particularly more likely to engage in confrontative and destructive offenses" (p. 718). Summarizing a large body of research on the relationship between peer relationships and aggressive behavior, Newcomb, Bukowski, & Pattee (1993) concluded that: "A clear consensus exists among social developmental researchers that children's peer relations provide unique and essential contributions to social and emotional development…rejected children were found to be more aggressive" (pp. 99, 114–115).

Researchers have ignored the relationship between school transitions and school violence, including bullying. However, Anderman and Kimweli (1997), notes "the transition from elementary to middle school during early adolescence is often associated with negative changes in achievement, attitudes, and motivation" (p. 8). Moreover, they suggest that the "timing of the school transition is less important than *the type of environment that the students move into*" [emphasis added] (p. 9). In other words, the school culture or environment may be conducive to violence. Specifically, the researchers found that violence was more prevalent in schools: (a) that engaged in practices incompatible with the developmental needs of students, (b) that had environments perceived by students as unsafe, and (c) where students perceived the quality of teaching as poor. Of these three factors, Anderman and Kimweli found that "*the most noteworthy effects were for perceiving the school as being unsafe*" [emphasis added] (p. 29).

This finding is consistent with Maslow's hierarchy of needs. According to Maslow (1973), human beings are motivated to satisfy their needs, which are "organized in to a hierarchy of relative prepotency" (p. 157). Human motivation begins with physiological needs—followed by the need for safety, love, and self-esteem—and culminating with the need for self-actualization. Each need emerges and becomes more important in human motivation as lower needs are satisfied progressively. When a basic need is unmet, however, it can become an all-consuming preoccupation. The result, according to Maslow, is that "the [individual's] whole philosophy of the future tends also to change" (p. 156). In other words, the unmet need becomes the central organizing principle for behavior and the cognitive framework for interpreting the world. Everything is interpreted in terms of satisfying the unmet need. All other concerns are subordinated to meeting this need.

The need for safety, the second most fundamental need in Maslow's hierarchy, is of particular relevance to a discussion of school violence and school transitions. Every student has an intrinsic need to feel safe. Persistent bullying, which threatens a student's physical, social, and psychological safety, may trigger an emergency response in the form of violence. For example, (Maslow 1973) writes that:

> Danger to these [basic needs] is reacted to almost as if it were a direct danger to the basic needs themselves. Such conditions as...freedom to defend one's self, justice, fairness, honesty, orderliness in the group are examples of such preconditions for basic need satisfaction. *Thwarting in these freedoms will be reacted to with a threat or emergency response* [emphasis added]. (p. 163)

The bullied student, whose safety, love, and self-esteem needs are relentlessly threatened, may lash out against all perceived perpetrators or co-conspirators. Like a cornered animal, the victim of a bully may see violence as the only means of self-protection. Alternatively, the bullied student may withdraw becoming increasingly marginalized and at increased risk of dropping out of school—mentally and physically.

Therefore, it is imperative that school safety be addressed as an integral part of any transition program. Although Anderman and Kimweli (1997) focus on the elementary to middle school transition, Morgan, (1999) argues that the strategies to assist transition to the middle school are applicable to the high school transition. In essence, although the intensity of the problem may vary by student age and grade level, the underlying problems and strategies needed to reduce school violence are similar. *Hence, an essential component of any successful transition strategy must be to ensure that students perceive the school environment that they will be entering as safe—free from bullying and other forms of violence.*

The place to begin is by taking bullying and other forms of student-to-student harassment seriously. School officials should begin by establishing a school culture that will not tolerate any form of harassment. Just as "zero-tolerance" policies have been established for weapons and drugs, a "zero-tolerance" policy should be established for bullying and other forms of peer-to-peer harassment. Administrators should establish clear expectations and sanctions and communicate those to the school community, beginning with students. Teachers and students should be taught to take even small acts of unkindness, verbal abuse, or any other form of harassment or bullying seriously. By focusing on small, seemingly insignificant acts of unkindness and bullying, administrators and teachers set an expectation and standard for interpersonal relationships and conflict resolution.

Second, school administration should establish a social relations training program. In a study designed to measure the effectiveness of comprehensive social relations intervention programs in reducing aggressive behavior among children, Lochman, Coie, Underwood, and Terry (1993) found "significant reductions in aggression and social rejection and improvements in peer prosocial behavior." The authors noted that the findings are of particular importance "because it is the aggressive, rejected subgroup of children that is at the greatest risk for negative adolescent outcomes. Thus, the children most in need of intervention were those who were significantly affected by this social relations program" (p. 1057). The program suggested by Lochman, et al. is comprised of four components: (a) social problem solving; (b) positive play training; (c) group-entry skill training; and (d) dealing effectively with strong negative feelings.

Third, school personnel need to take character education seriously and infuse it throughout the school's culture and curriculum. Character education is not a separate course; it is the sum total of school culture, of what is taught in the classroom as right and wrong, of the rewards and sanctions given for certain behaviors, and by what teachers and administrators model. In other words, educators should strive to create schools that have a civilizing affect on students. Children have a natural proclivity toward egocentrism, crudeness, defiance of authority, and aggression. If not corrected and restrained by the socializing and civilizing affects of parental guidance, social pressure, and good schooling, students will be caught in a web of bullying or victimization that will increase their risk of dropping out of school or of underachieving.

Fourth, schools must take concrete steps to reduce the incidence of bullying. Hazler (1994, 39–40) suggests several administrative steps. They recommend that school personnel should:

1. Recognize bullying as a serious problem, and not look the other way;

2. Deal directly with the problem and take action immediately;

3. Get parents involved and communicate to students' parents that the staff won't tolerate harassment of any kind;

4. Create appropriate activities (i.e., awareness activities help students focus on understanding how victims, bullies, and witnesses feel, and why they act the way they do);

5. Develop classroom action plans in which the students agree to specific actions they can take to lessen the problems in their class or at the school;

6. Hold regular discussion with their students (i.e., discussing examples of bullying from history and current events in class can be effective);

7. Teach cooperation and encourage group work; and

8. Provide appropriate professional counseling as necessary.

In short, any successful transition program will reduce student fears concerning safety issues by adopting comprehensive policies designed to ensure that schools are largely free of bullying, harassment, and other forms of violence. When students feel safe, they can focus on building positive relationships and academic achievement and will be less likely to drop out of school, underachieve, or get into trouble.

9

Ninth-Grade Transitions and Improvements

There is no doubt that the transition between middle school and high school is a difficult one for many teenagers. In virtually every high school, the ninth grade accounts for the largest number of students who demonstrate poor attendance, accumulate tardies, and cause disturbances and disruptions. A few ninth graders are suspended or expelled; many fail to earn enough credits to be promoted to the tenth grade. Ninth graders usually account for most of the dropouts as well. In many school districts, relations between middle level and high school educators deteriorate because each blames the other for the new ninth grade problem (George and McEwin 1999). Now high school educators are realizing that the inclusion of ninth-grade students in the senior high school is likely to be permanent. Educators realize that "keeping the students at the middle school until they are ready" is not a long-term solution to their immaturity. In the last ten years, high school educators have invested time and energy into ways to improve the transition from middle school to high school.

Ninth graders in August are academically, physically, socially, and emotionally not much different than they were as eighth graders in June. Yet, high school teachers expect these students to make an immediate adjustment to a different school setting. High schools are generally departmentalized with little team teaching. Homerooms are set up primarily to take attendance and to disseminate information about school events. High school educators expect ninth grade students to suppress their natural energy in order to adapt and conform to an organizational structure that is perhaps best suited for 17- and 18-year-old students (Jett, Pulling, and Ross 1994).

The high expectation for eighth graders to make an immediate adjustment to high school places unnecessary pressure on these youngest high school students. Many times the personal behaviors, values, and norms of ninth graders may be established and reinforced by upperclassmen. High school teachers must understand that the transition is hard for all ninth graders. These students have newfound freedom. They are able to walk where they want to during breaks. Peer pressure sometimes causes students to make poor personal decisions. As eighth graders they were the oldest students, but now they find are the youngest as ninth graders on campus. This new adaptation forces them to find ways to fit in, or they eventually drop out. High school administrators, counselors, and teachers can do many positive things to support, assist, and nurture incoming ninth graders. While negative peer pressure cannot be altogether eliminated, it can be minimized with proper attention.

First, to build relationships with new students, high school teachers need to attend eighth-grade meetings to learn about the different students in each class. This is important for curriculum alignment as well. They can become aware of the educational, social, and emotional needs their future students. Eighth-grade students might be invited to the high school periodically to participate in classes with ninth graders. Upperclassmen could work at the middle schools as tutors or teacher aides. Through such activities, eighth-grade students begin to view the high school in a positive manner. In return, the high school teachers learn to appreciate the eighth-grade student. As a result, they can provide activities to welcome and support the middle school students.

Second, principals and their staffs should consider going to block scheduling. This schedule allows students to have only four classes each semester in 90-minute blocks. The block schedule allows teachers more freedom in the classroom to use alternative teaching strategies. The biggest advantage for safer schools and incoming freshmen is that students have less class changes on a daily basis. Merely the fact that students are in the halls less will reduce the amount of violence that occurs on the campus.

Third, schools should set up advisement programs. Guidance counselors are assigned a wide range of duties. Advisement groups directed by teachers for freshmen could help students adjust to high school and help prepare them for cultural and educational differences in the school. Even though ninth graders readily embrace the newly discovered freedoms of high school, if they are left to exercise this freedom without guidance from staff members, they may make poor choices about both their social life and their academic studies. An advisory program that meets during the homeroom period can help students make better decisions.

Teachers can provide students with information and advice while monitoring their academic progress as well. Advisors can facilitate dialogue among students about important decisions students are faced with such as relationships with families and friends, using drugs and alcohol, engaging in sexual behavior, or becoming involved in violent and criminal behavior. Through the advisement program, educators can help provide a safe, secure, and supportive environment. Teachers can build self-esteem and self-confidence in their students. Many educators believe that advisement programs provide a positive alternative to the "lure of the street" and emphasize individual care and concern for each student (Daly 1996).

Fourth, educators can assign well-trained upperclassman as mentors for ninth graders. Many times ninth graders feel isolated because of their status as incoming freshmen. Older students can take these most vulnerable students under their wing. Freshmen can seek advice from older students during the advisement period. A well-trained mentor could truly be a "life molder."

Fifth, some school districts establish a three-week summer course designed to help eighth graders transition smoothly to high school. During this course, incoming students receive an orientation to the school and community. They participate in a special curriculum that promotes student bonding and thematic learning (Gallager and Satter 1998).

Finally, schools can create opportunities for ninth graders to participate in non-competitive games as a part of their school program. Ninth graders should be provided opportunities to act like 13- and 14-year-old adolescents. The competitive pressure to achieve first place causes feelings of anxiety, self-doubt, and fear for many freshman students. Such feelings can affect the behavior of any age student; these worries seem to especially affect students who are in transition from middle to high school. Competitive activities can be balanced with non-competitive "fun" activities for freshman. In these activities, all students can participate, regardless of skill level. They can establish and nurture interpersonal relationships without the risk of feeling like a "loser" in front of their peer group. The entire school can benefit from intramural programs for all students.

High school staff members should recognize that 13- and 14-year-old students have different emotional, physical, and social needs than older high school students. Unless opportunities are created within the high school for younger students to naturally express themselves, they will mimic the behaviors of older students. In doing so, they may suppress healthy feelings that might lead to delays in their academic, social, and emotional development. Ultimately, these delays in their healthy growth could cause behavior problems that have severe consequences.

Discipline and Transitions

Schools with good discipline and high success rates for ninth-grade transitions hold programs, strategies, and philosophies that support and value student responsibility and proper citizenship as fundamental components of good discipline. Most students come to high school each day to be successfully engaged in the excellent instructional programs and services that are available to them. However, the inappropriate actions of a few individuals can cloud the overall "good" of the educational programs (Peterson and Skiba 2000). Learning cannot take place in an atmosphere of fear or intimidation. The misdeeds of one student can hamper the learning of an entire class. If a school is going to help ninth graders adapt successfully, it must understand the mechanics of a well-disciplined school.

Ninth graders must understand that well-disciplined schools have clear and concise curriculum goals. The school is totally student-oriented in its focus. Programs are instituted for the benefit of the students and staff members. New students must understand their roles as student advocates. Whenever students misbehave the symptoms and causes are reviewed and addressed by concerned adults. All student management programs emphasize positive student behaviors, student responsibility, and preventative measures rather than punitive actions. Well-disciplined high schools would rather catch students "doing something right" than catch them "doing something wrong." In a well-disciplined school, staff members must value the partnership with students and must provide them with opportunities to help solve campus-wide problems. This cooperative environment is important to demonstrate the belief that students and teachers, working together, can accomplish more. No one person can make a school successful (Hill 1996). Ninth graders must learn that well-disciplined schools are sensitive to their students' racial and social-economic concerns. Everyone must understand how these concerns are manifested in the instructional program. All ninth graders are informed and aware of their rights and responsibilities as citizens in a democratic society and as a member of the high school. Intervention strategies—such as teacher discussions, informal counseling, parent contacts, formal counseling, detentions and suspensions—are available as needed (Heller 1996).

Through working with the eighth grade team, staff members can identify at-risk students and gather a wide array of intervention strategies based on the needs of each individual student. These students are encouraged and counseled to become a part of the school's rigorous academic and co-curricular programs. When it comes to student management, students should be recognized for positive behaviors. Ninth graders must understand that consistency is the key to a successful intervention program. They must understand that they will be treated fairly with moral values being a major part of each decision.

Violence Prevention Programs

As high schools become more complex, they are faced with larger issues daily. Young freshmen are walking into an entirely new culture. Many schools have implemented violence prevention programs in response to the increasing violent behavior among students. The types of programs vary, emphasizing such diverse elements as: metal detectors, resource officers, guest speakers, teacher training in self-defense, anger management classes for students, and mediation processes. Some programs show videotapes of encounters and contain structured conversations about how fights start and alternative ways of managing that aggression (Johnson and Johnston 1996). Peer mediation has been adopted widely by school systems across the nation (Tyrell, Scully, and Halligan 1998). This program provides an opportunity for trained student mediators who work with faculty facilitators to assist students in resolving their complaints with other students. The mediators strive for a mutually acceptable resolution that is signed by all involved parties. Students may volunteer for peer mediation or it may be mandated by the administration. The following six steps must be implemented in order for the program to achieve success. First, the program must be introduced into a cooperative context. Students must work together and trust one another in mediating through a problem. Through this cooperative learning concept, students can handle disputes constructively. Second, students must understand that many conflicts have positive outcomes. To deny, suppress, repress, or ignore conflicts in an attempt to eliminate violence is a mistake. Students need to be taught that *managed* conflicts should occur more often to offset the potential of violence. Third, students must be taught a specific procedure for negotiating agreements. Students must be able to: define what the problem is, describe the feelings of all involved, see underlying causes, and generate three optional agreements that would satisfy both parties. Fourth, students must be taught the rules of the mediation process. They must make sure that all hostilities are dissolved before the mediators facilitate negotiations between the two parties and formalize an agreement. Fifth, the peer mediation program must be implemented slowly. Initially, working in pairs to develop the necessary communication skills will enable them to become successful facilitators. Sixth, the training must continue weekly to refine and upgrade student skills. The process to becoming a competent mediator is on going.

Peer mediation programs supplement discipline programs by modeling for students the format and skills they need to regulate their own behaviors. All students must learn how to manage their conflicts in a constructive manner. Training students how to negotiate and mediate will ensure that future generations are prepared to manage conflicts in their careers, families, and communities. Ninth graders can learn mature methods for coping with peer conflict in the high school setting. High school students who master the skills of negotiation and mediation have a developmental advantage over their peers who have not gained those skills.

10

Examining Exemplar Programs

Safe schools and student transition into high school are two of the largest issues facing educators in secondary education today. Along with curriculum improvements, principals must continually strive to find ways to show young adults that communication and collaboration are the keys to avoiding conflicts. Educators who have lived and worked with ninth graders believe that the transition year between middle level and high school is one of the most exciting, turbulent, and important years in the maturation of young people. Educational leaders must find ways to address the "whole child" if they are going to help students grow emotionally, socially, and educationally.

One midwestern high school is taking proactive and constructive steps to help all students, particularly ninth graders, strengthen their relationships with their peers. Their program focuses on improving the entire school environment as a significant way to enhance student's wellness and safety. When students and faculty members nourish inviting relationships, caring communities are developed within the school. Schools that implement only measures—such as metal detectors, student identification badges, and locker inspections—have confined themselves to solutions that are problematic. However, if schools include practices that promote cooperation, teach conflict resolution, highlight the value of service to others, encourage empathy, and promote belonging and trust, they can truly create safe schools (Gallager and Satter 1998).This school district in Kansas City initiated a school wellness program that grew each year. The *Impact Program* is a total wellness and awareness initiative that provides students with a support network of peers, teachers, parents, and school and community programs. It is designed to recognize troubling trends and respond to societal changes that can consume the lives of youth and cause them to drop out of school. The ultimate goal is to provide students with the necessary skills to be healthy adults. The Impact Program has a variety of student activities that help students view cooperation and communication as the keys to solving conflicts.

Project ALERT is a fourteen-lesson drug prevention program for students in grades 6, 7, and 8 that has dramatically reduced experimentation, as well as regular drug use among adolescents (Hertzog and Morgan 1999). This program focuses on the substances that adolescents use first and most widely: alcohol, tobacco, marijuana, and inhalants. Project ALERT uses participatory activities and videos to help students establish non-drug norms, develop reasons not to use, and resist pro-drug pressures. Guided classroom discussions and small group activities stimulate peer interaction and challenge students, while intensive role-playing encourages students to practice and master resistance skills. Parent-involved homework assignments extend the learning process.

Project ALERT is a highly acclaimed program endorsed by the National Middle School Association, honored by the National Prevention Network, and recognized by the White House Office of National Drug Control Policy (1999). The goals of Project ALERT (1999) are explicit: (a) to prevent adolescents from beginning to use drugs, and to prevent those who have already experimented from becoming regular users; and (b) to prevent or curb risk factors that have been demonstrated to predict drug use. The curriculum achieves these goals by motivating adolescents not to use drugs and by teaching them skills to transfer their motivation into effective resistance. The lessons that focus on norms, beliefs about drugs, and intentions help motivate adolescents not to use drugs. Those that focus on how to identify and resist pressures stemming from the availability of drugs and pressures to use, stress skills. The proximal goal of each lesson is clearly stated in the introduction and is reinforced in the conclusion of the lesson.

Project ALERT is highly effective with middle-school adolescents aged 11 to 14 years from widely divergent backgrounds and communities. The program has been successful with high- and low-risk youth from urban, rural, and suburban communities; with youth from different socioeconomic levels; and with whites, African Americans, Latinos, and Asian Americans.

Researchers have found that when middle-school students took part in a high school transition program with several diverse articulation activities, fewer students were retained in the transition grade and fewer students were expected to drop out before graduation when the school provided supportive advisory group activities or responsive remediation programs. Studies by Oates and colleagues (1998) found that students involved in a comprehensive program at Sunrise Middle School in inner-city Philadelphia were more successful in their transition into high school than students who had not participated in the *Community for Learning Program* (CFL). The key components of this program are: support and training for teachers; a learning management system designed to help middle school students develop a sense of responsibility for their own learning and behavior; and an emphasis on community and family involvement.

Ninth grade is a fragile and confusing time for young people who may experience troubles ranging from issues of sex, drugs, violence, and/or family problems. A system-wide effort to combat dropout rates and acts of violence in Detroit, Michigan, focuses on ninth graders and efforts to provide them extra guidance (Reinhard 1997). Ninth-grade students in Detroit study a basic curriculum and attend most of their classes in one wing of the school building, making it easier for them to find their teachers and to avoid tangling with older students. In the 1960s, concerns about providing a more supportive environment for early adolescents fueled the middle school movement, which advocated replacing junior-high schools serving grades seven to nine with middle schools comprising grades six to eight. That transformation shifted most ninth graders from junior highs to high schools.

Detroit pays for its ninth-grade program with $16 million per year in state at-risk and federal Title I money aimed at educating poor children (1999). Most programs are modeled after one at Kettering High, which enrolls between 400 and 500 ninth graders per year. In the spring, Kettering starts gathering information from its feeder middle schools about eighth graders with poor grades, poor attendance, and family problems. Those students, usually about one-fourth of the class, are invited to attend a five-week summer session to give them a glimpse of what they'll study in high school and what they'll need to do to graduate from high school. The four-hour days include innovative instruction, such as building model cars, calculating distances, and learning about Newton's laws of gravity and motion through writing compositions. Administrators in Detroit have found that these students do better if they get a head start on everyone else.

Freshman Transition, an orientation program for freshmen at East Hartford High School in Connecticut, provides teachers and administrators the opportunity to go over rules, guidelines, and school programs that promote: proper work habits, honesty, dependability, the ability to get along with others, and the development of positive citizenship traits (Hertzog and Morgan 1999). Specific programs at East Hartford include the *Interdisciplinary Enrichment Academic Program* (IDEA), *Advisor/Advisee* and *Mentor/Mentee* Programs, *Parent Involvement* and *Ninth Grade Transition* Programs. The Ninth Grade Transition Program targets at-risk students, providing academic tutoring and support from a full-time staff member.

Additional exemplary practices used in high schools to improve transitions and school violence are listed below:

1. *Anger Management Seminars* teach socially appropriate skills to help students deal with anger in a constructive manner.

2. *HUG Program—Human Understanding and Growth Program* provides workshops for small groups of students on a regular basis. They discuss adolescent development and other sensitive issues (human sexuality, drug abuse, peer pressure) with their peers.

3. *Pair Program* involves voluntary staff members acting as instructional resources in a "big brother/big sister" type of program.

4. *Peer Mediation,* discussed earlier, involves students helping to mediate conflicts between classmates.

5. *Pupil Personnel Services (Dropout Prevention Team)* involves guidance counselors working with community members to identify at-risk students and evaluate their achievement in order to determine possible strategies to help the student be successful.

6. *Current Staff Development* provides teachers with updated strategies on student management. Several faculty meetings each year are devoted to helping staff members identify potential problems and intervene in appropriate and effective ways.

7. *SAVE—Students Against Violence Everywhere* is a program that helps students work with local police agencies in order to find ways to decrease violence in the schools and communities.

8. *Improv* is a program composed of student groups who perform skits with wellness themes for elementary children. They receive information on controversial issues and devise a skit. After the performance, they facilitate open discussions about the issues (Gallager and Satter 1998).

9. *SADD—Students Against Destructive Decisions* is a program designed to raise student awareness concerning the consequences of drinking and driving.

10. *Hi-Step* is a high school student-taught elementary program involving cross-age teaching. In this program, high school students teach fourth graders about peer pressure, peer mediation, drug abuse, and relationships.

11. *PAL—Peers Always Listen* is a group of students available to listen and to help their peers sort out their problems, without giving advice.

12. *High School Heroes* are groups of teenagers who teach tobacco awareness to elementary students

13. *Establishment of Advisement Groups* is accomplished by dividing students into small homeroom groups that will help students in their academic, social, and cognitive growth. Advisors lead

discussions on important issues at each grade level that help students adapt to high school and their community.

Effective and comprehensive transition programs help: to build a sense of community; to respond to the needs and concerns of students; and to provide appropriate, multifaceted approaches in order to facilitate the transition process. When asked about their concerns in facing a school transition from middle to high school, students in Gwinnett County, Georgia, listed—among others concerns—the following: (a) getting to class on time; (b) finding lockers; (c) getting through the crowded halls; and (d) encountering the aggressive and violent behaviors of other students. Empirical evidence suggests that middle schools tend to emphasize relative ability and competition among students more, and effort and improvement less. This middle school emphasis leads to a decline in task goals, ability goals, and academic efficacy.

11

Developing an Effective Transitional Plan for the Local School System

The following guidelines have been successful and well tested for planning transition programs (Weldy 1991). Local school systems should:

1. Provide several activities that will involve students, parents, teachers, and staff from both schools in the transition process;

2. Establish a transition protocol that can be easily replicated and updated annually;

3. Establish a timeline for the transition process;

4. Schedule meetings between collaborative groups from the sending and the receiving schools and schedule discussions for adults and students about the issues;

5. Assess the human and financial resources available to support the transition process; and

6. Ask students, teachers, guidance counselors, parents, and others to evaluate the transition program.

Effective middle-level transition programs establish a sense of belonging among the multiple constituencies involved, appropriately respond to the needs of the incoming students, and provide multiple opportunities for all constituencies to develop a meaningful role during the transition process as well as maintain that role throughout the school year.

Many different types of violence prevention programs exist which focus on transitions from middle to high schools. Determining what type of program, or combination of program components, is best for a particular school requires an assessment of the school's circumstances, student body, and resources. Assessments must continue as the program operates so that changes can be made to account for new development and to improve outcomes. Such evaluation data can then be used to support requests for funding the program's continuation. In an intervention program, three questions should be addressed: (a) What are the program's results and what does it change? (b) What program qualities make it work effectively? and (c) Is the program cost effective? The evaluation should focus on needs assessments, outcome evaluations, process or monitoring evaluations, and cost-benefit analysis.

An orderly, disciplined and safe school depends on a comprehensive consideration of the total environment and climate of the school that is based on physical, social, and academic factors, as well as the school-community relationship. In a study conducted to examine the perceptions of school violence held by pre-service teachers, practicing teachers, and students at middle and high school levels, the middle school group responded with more concerns and fears of school violence (Young and Craig 1999). School children, aged 14–17, are most at-risk of gun violence in schools with 25 percent of the violent acts occurring in the hallways and nearly 19 percent in the classrooms (Suarez 1992). In 1990, 36 percent of ninth and twelfth grade males, 12 percent of ninth grade females, and 9 percent of twelfth grade females in North Carolina public schools reported carrying weapons for their protection. Most of these reported weapons were knives and razors, but about 12 percent of the males and 3 percent of the females reported carrying handguns (Suarez 1992). Literature on school safety indicates a safe school is both a condition for and an outcome of an effective school. Educators can ease the fears and address the problem of safe schools: by providing challenging and supportive middle school environments; by designing transition programs that address the needs of students and their parents; and by facilitating communication between middle school and high school educators (Mizelle 1999).

Adolescence is a time of change in many domains of an individual's life. One change in particular occurs when many middle schools transition from oftentimes a smaller middle school to a larger, more diverse high school. As the change in academics occurs, many adolescents will experience biological and social changes which all have reciprocal effects on the individual. Upon entering high school, adolescents will encounter significant changes in the size of their classrooms and the number of teachers they encounter as they simultaneously are developing cognitive skills of abstract and hypothetical reasoning (Steinberg 1996). Balance between home and school is important in both facilitating and supporting the academic endeavors of the individual. It is critical that the development of an effective transitional program for middle school students as they enter high school involve a large base of support including, students, teachers, parents, administrators, and community members and leaders.

The recommended sequence of safe school planning begins with developing a climate for action. Assessing the attitudes of the various district and school-site personnel, community agencies, and the community-at-large about school violence and the need to provide support for middle school students as they begin their high school years are both equally important in the development of a transition program. This assessment can be measured through a survey or by simply talking with groups of students, parents, teachers, and community members. If the attitudes toward safety and change are positive, the planning process will be an easy one. If negative attitudes toward change exist, they should be known early so that they can be addressed. In creating and maintaining a positive climate for review and action, it is important to enlist the support of everyone concerned and to foster that support throughout the ongoing process of planning, implementing, and evaluating. The superintendent and other district administrators must be involved and supportive from the beginning of the planning process. Members of local governing boards and the law enforcement and juvenile justice community also should be approached as important allies in the planning process. The climate for action will be maintained and continued with these groups aware and supportive of the planning necessary for a safe school and a smooth transition into high school.

The initial steps of the planning process must focus on the development of a climate in the school and a community that supports critical evaluation and pursuing appropriate actions. A broad-based committee should be established to develop the transition plan, with specific interest on the issue of school violence. If there is an existing School Improvement Program or Leadership Team already established in the system, there is no need to form an additional group. This team will be familiar with working together towards a common goal; and with a few additional members who possess expertise in middle schools or school violence, the team should provide a broad enough base to develop a comprehensive transition plan. Group leaders of the planning team must strive to acknowledge and harmonize the diversity of concerns and expectations individuals bring to the planning process. The better the planning committee deals with these elements of teambuilding, the better its school safety plan will be.

Determining goals of the transition program may begin with strategy planning techniques, such as brainstorming visions and objectives for such a program. Establishing broad goals for the transition plan that constitute the shared vision of the school and community serves as a common starting point for the planning process. As the desired outcomes are identified and consensus is achieved, the vision binds together each member of the school and community, and the various aspects of change into a coordinated whole. This process should result in a written statement representing the shared vision and a list of specific goals and objectives. Studies of existing programs should be analyzed and reviewed to help establish the specific goals. For example, studies by Mizelle (1995) found that students who stayed together with the same teachers through middle school grades—experiencing more hands-on, life-related learning activities, integrated instruction, and cooperative learning groups—were more successful in their transition to high school than were students from the same school who had a more traditional middle school experience.

According to MacIver (1990), an effective transition program from middle to high school should include a variety of activities that: (a) provide students and parents with information about the new school; (b) provide students with social support during the transition; and (c) bring middle and high school personnel together to learn about one another's curriculum and requirements. To plan improvements, it is necessary to understand the existing conditions at the school. The analysis of these conditions should be based on a collection of quantitative data, such as school-crime reporting statistics, attendance records, and truancy data, as well as on qualitative data, such as attitude surveys of teachers, parents, students, and community members. Middle school students want to know what high school is going to be like, and they and their parents need to know about and understand high school programs and procedures (Phelan, Yu, and Davidson 1994). Some of the ways students can learn about high school include: visiting the high school in the spring, attending a presentation by a high school student or panel of students, or discussing high school regulations and procedures with eighth-grade teachers and counselors.

A transition program should include activities that will provide incoming students social support activities that give students the opportunity to get to know and develop positive relationships with older students and incoming students. Examples of this could be a *Big Sister/Big Brother Program* that begins in the eighth grade and continues through ninth grade, a spring social event for current and incoming high school students, and writing programs where eighth-graders correspond with high school students. More long-term activities, such as peer mentoring and tutoring programs, should also be considered for implementation. Middle and high school educators should collaborate to learn about the programs, courses, curriculum, and requirements of the sending and receiving schools.

Existing records and reports that are regularly produced by schools, law enforcement, juvenile justice, and other social agencies should be analyzed for input into the planning process of the transition program. Records such as standard student crime reporting records, suspension and expulsion records, attendance and truancy data, and student progress reports should be studied to predict patterns and needs of the most pressing safety issues confronting the school. Efforts to gather information on the schools involved in the transition process will help the planning committee stay focused on the specific needs involved for both the middle and high schools.

The actual planning process of the transition program should be a part of the overall planning and evaluation process already established in the school. The next steps should involve identifying priorities and objectives, implementing activities, and evaluating the plan. Although the specific process each transition committee uses to make decisions will vary, the following tasks must be accomplished during this stage of planning. The committee needs to:

1. Determine which concerns and needs are the highest priorities;

2. Explore the possible causes of safety concerns;

3. Identify resources needed and available;

4. Develop possible strategies and actions; and

5. Develop evaluation criteria and timelines.

In choosing actions for the transition plan, the committee should consider three levels of action planning: prevention, intervention, and restructuring. *Prevention* efforts are those actions and programs designed to prevent problems before they occur. Sample prevention actions might include adjusting the curriculum as East Hartford School in Connecticut did to provide varied programs for students to enable them to secure the type of education best suited to meet their particular needs, interests, and abilities (Hertzog and Morgan 1999). Proper work habits, honesty, dependability, the ability to get along with others, and the development of positive citizenship traits are also essential components of this Freshman Transition Program.

Intervention programs are actions and programs that are designed to reduce or eliminate already existing problems. Sample intervention actions at the Connecticut schools that have implemented transition programs include the Ninth Grade Transition Program, designed to reduce the ninth grade retention rate. Targeting at-risk students, this program provides academic tutoring while allowing the student to develop a connection to the high school through a relationship with a full-time staff member. Programs are designed to help at-risk students who do not graduate from the eighth grade and are socially promoted to the ninth. "Big Brothers and Sisters" are involved in many of the schools implementing a transition program, as well as Advisor/Advisee programs, parent groups, reentry programs for dropouts, gang violence and drug suppression programs, and training for staff in conflict resolution and group problem-solving.

Efforts designed for *restructuring* are long-term, comprehensive programs designed to reorganize a problem school, including changing attitudes and beliefs of the school community members. Sample restructuring actions might include a comprehensive combination of homerooms offering specialized instruction (non-violence, self-esteem, conflict resolution, and drug and alcohol education); regular off-site staff development sessions for teachers and support personnel; school-wide policies on homework, dress, and conduct; regular involvement of law enforcement and juvenile justice personnel on campus with students and staff; and student assemblies confronting issues like gangs, multicultural relations, drugs, and self-esteem.

In the middle grades, students make personal and educational decisions with serious consequences. They wrestle with issues of authority, independence, changing family relationships, and increased visibility in the community, all of which require that students practice social skills for community participation. Schools can create programs that respond to the unique needs of middle-grade students and families. Communities can publicize positive reports about middle-grade students and provide positive interventions for middle-grade students. Schools alone can't solve problems with complex societal origins. Experts agree that comprehensive efforts involving schools, community groups, and local agencies are much more effective. Some schools are working with local businesses to provide job-related programs for high-risk youths. Experts and common sense indicate the importance of reaching kids before gangs and other harmful groups. "Gang pre-vention" curricula have been developed in many middle schools around the nation, with studies indicating student changes in atti-tudes towards gangs.

The evaluation of programs and activities is the final step in developing a successful transition program. Evaluation can inform effective implementation of a program; can enable a school to demonstrate the value of the program to the community, to parents, and to potential funding sources; and can influence the formation and implementation of social policy, both locally and nationally

A needs assessment (or formative evaluation) helps a school determine its critical needs, including violence reduction and pre-vention. The following questions might help a school develop a more effective long-term strategy dealing with school violence and middle-school transition (Flannery 1998):

1. What is the nature and prevalence of violence and victimiza-tion at the school or in the neighborhood?

2. What is the impact of violence on the children's adjustment, mental health, and learning?

3. What is the extent of gang activity at school?

The second type of evaluation is called outcome evaluation. It answers the questions:

1. What changed because of the intervention?

2. Did the program reduce the children's problem behavior, aggression, delinquency, and violence?

3. Did the program increase student attendance and improve school grades?

4. Did it result in reduced discipline visits to the principal's office?

5. Did it result in increased social competence or improved social skills?

Being clear about what the program is meant to address (and not address) is essential to measuring its effectiveness. Some popular programs may be effective in changing some problem behaviors but may not result in decreased student violence. Some of the factors that underlie problem behaviors in children are shared by intervention strategies: improving problem-solving and conflict resolution skills, increasing attachment to school and success at school, and improving communication and social skills. These are valuable targets of intervention for most students in most schools. The targets of intervention must be clearly explicated if they are to serve as the focus of the transition program. The reasons these are desired outcomes and the manner in which they relate to reductions in aggressive behavior, conflict, or violence must be clearly stated. This requires a clear understanding of the risk factors the school is attempting to ameliorate or the protective factors it is trying to promote. Clearly defining program goals and desired outcomes will greatly affect the establishment of relevant and effective outcome assessments of the program's success, and will help to identify possible limitations of the program as well.

The third type of evaluation is a process evaluation. Process evaluation attempts to address the question, "What works best about our program and why does it work?" Is program effectiveness related to: the quality of teacher or staff training; the number of years an individual has been teaching; strong administration support for the program; the scope of the program; or active parent involvement in program implementation and support? Flannery and Torquati (1993) found that teachers believed that parents volunteering in the classroom was the biggest factor in determining the program's success for students, even more important than administrative support, the quality of teacher training, and the teacher's own "buy in" of the program's importance and effectiveness.

The last type of basic evaluation is cost-benefit analysis. It might include an assessment of how much the program costs to implement per student or school, or how much the program saves in other related costs. Schools can utilize many techniques as part of an evaluation strategy. Many different kinds of information are readily available to schools for low cost and effort. Potential sources of information include self-reports by the students, teachers, parents, and principals. Most schools collect archival data as part of their everyday operations (attendance, grades, conduct ratings on report cards, disciplinary contacts, suspension, weapons, violations, visits to the nurse's office for treatment of injury, costs to repair vandalism and property destruction). Schools may also partner with local police or sheriff's departments to gather aggregate data on community crime and the nature or types of contacts children from their school have with the police.

There are three basic components to any evaluation that will make the results more readily interpretable and valid (Flannery 1998). The first is the collection of outcome data prior to implementation of the intervention. This information provides the school with a baseline of student behavior, grades, attendance, etc., from which to determine change at a later time. The second is assessment, whenever possible, of a comparison group of students (or classrooms or schools) not exposed to the intervention or program. A comparison group will allow a determination of if and how the intervention is effective for children in the program as opposed to those not in the program.

The third component of an effective evaluation design is random assignment of students to treatment groups or controls. This is the most difficult to achieve, practically and ethically, and may not be possible in most situations. Random assignment of two equally deserving children, with similar assessments of both children, provide the strongest evidence that it was the treatment that caused any observed differences in a child's outcome. One strategy that has been used successfully is random assignment of students to control groups or treatments at the beginning of an evaluation, with eventual provision of the same treatment to the controls. If a whole school is in a comparison group, then all students in the school continue to receive the same services and attention. If the control is an individual student, it is harder to justify withholding the treatment. This is especially true when the treatment may address a very serious, immediate, and potentially dangerous problem like violence.

Violence among youth, especially in middle and high schools, is one of American society's most pressing concerns. It is also a source of controversy. While no recent nationwide study concerning the real extent of youth violence is available, small-scale and regional studies indicate that youth violence is increasing, at least slightly. In addition, youth, like adults, are now more frequently using guns instead of fists to settle disputes. Recent studies indicate that the most prevalent type of youth crime is theft, and the most common types of violence are fistfights, bullying, and shoving matches. Gang activity at school is particularly susceptible to "the Ostrich syndrome," as administrators may ignore the problem. Unfortunately, there is also sometimes a contradiction between school policies and practice. This creates a situation where teachers do not feel supported when they impose discipline, students do not feel protected, and the violence-prone think they will not be punished.

Community activities frequently focus on breaking family cycles of violence. The most effective are long-term interventions providing a range of family services. They involve the collaborative efforts of religious and recreational organizations; social service, public housing and health agencies; the business community; the schools; and law enforcement agencies. Programs in parenting skills and family relationships, particularly those focusing on nonviolent living skills and recovery from substance abuse, can protect children from learning violence at home. Out-of-school programs keep youth constructively engaged when their families are unavailable and provide caring adults and good role models. Helping youth find employment and community campaigns to supplement school programs against gangs are crucial to the middle to high school transition program.

Concern about increasing youth violence is being channeled into a variety of innovative, and potentially effective, programs around the country. Although components vary depending on the particular needs of the community and school, the most effective transition programs (Schwartz 1996):

- Make an accurate assessment of the existence of violence and, especially, gang activity;

- Use all the resources in the community, including social service and law enforcement, and do not just rely on school officials to deal with the problem;

- Incorporate family services into both community and school programs;

- Intervene early in a child's life;

- Include not only anti-violence strategies but also positive experiences;

- Create and communicate clearly defined behavior codes, and enforce them strictly and uniformly; and

- Prepare to engage in a long-term effort.

Early evaluations of well-organized programs suggest that success is possible, though; and statistics demonstrating an increase in youth violence, however slight, indicate that the effort and expenditure are necessary.

The development of effective transition programs for middle school students entering high school include initiatives such as teaming arrangements, at-risk programs, parent involvement initiatives, interdisciplinary enrichment programs, retreat experiences, and multi-cultural considerations. The primary mission of one Connecticut high school is to sustain and profit by a richly diverse environment that will enable all students: to develop those intellectual skills, to acquire the essential knowledge, and to develop the personal character needed to become responsible citizens capable of adapting and succeeding in a changing world (Hertzog and Morgan 1997). Programs are provided specifically for freshman students with the following beliefs in the forefront of all planning and development (1997).

- Every individual is unique and has worth.

- All individuals can learn.

- People learn best in a safe, nurturing, and healthy environment.

- Schools prepare students for the responsibility of citizenship in a democratic society.

- Learning is a life-long process.

- Education is a cooperative effort among students, teachers, parents, and the community at large.

- Individuals and organizations are accountable for their actions.

- Education and daily life are interconnected.

- Progress requires change.

Evaluations and assessment data from some of the schools in Connecticut suggest that the efforts of the transition programs have been extremely successful, not just for students but for the overall climate of the school (Hertzog and Morgan 1999). When comparing the ninth grade students who were "on teams" to the previous year's freshman who were not on teams, there was a decrease in the number of overall discipline referrals, and fewer in-school and out-of-school suspensions. Student attendance improved and there was an increase in the amount of communication with parents. Overall studies supported the individual school reports that the dropout rate was significantly lower for schools that implemented nine or more transition practices. Schools that fell into this category had a coordinated plan between the middle school and the high school and incorporated activities, such as mentoring programs, summer programs, and advisor/advisee programs. Evaluators of the Connecticut programs conclude that successful transition programs are programs that involve all of the stakeholders in the design and implementation. This includes eighth and ninth grade parents, teachers, administrators, counselors, and students. The key to successful transition is that transition is a process, not an event (1999).

Researchers know that when middle school students took part in a high school transition program with several diverse articulation activities, fewer students were retained in the transition grade (MacIver 1990). In addition, middle school principals indicated that they expected fewer of their students to drop out before graduation when the school provided supportive advisory group activities or responsive remediation programs. The overarching goals of some successful transition programs include (1990): (1) raising all students' levels of motivation and academic achievement; (2) promoting student success, respect, and responsibility while reaching for the future; (3) creating an environment that promotes social growth and development; (4) creating an instructional environment that promotes teachers interaction and supports student learning;

and (5) improving student management as related to academic expectations, attendance, and behavior. Enabling strategies include the following:

1. Use of course wide performance learning and assessment;

2. Use of cooperative learning;

3. Use of inter- and intra- disciplinary instruction;

4. Increase exposure for all students to a high level curriculum; and

5. Enhance monitoring of student performance and unified student interventions.

Schools should be safe for teaching and learning. It is incumbent upon policymakers, administrators, and community leaders to prepare for those unthinkable violent occurrences that happen all too often. The General Accounting Office of the U.S. Government identified seven components when developing a violence prevention program for schools (Reddick and Peach 1998). These seven components are:

1. A comprehensive approach that recognizes the complexity of violence;

2. An early start and long-term commitment;

3. Strong school leadership and clear, consistent discipline policies and procedures;

4. Training for administrators, teachers, and staff in behavior management, mediation, and violence prevention strategies;

5. Parent training and involvement;

6. Links to law enforcement and social service agencies and the community; and

7. Culturally sensitive and developmentally appropriate materials and activities for students.

The issue for providing safe schools is challenging and complex. Initiating programs and students services that will help to address comprehensive efforts to reduce violence in schools, such as the transition program, is a community-wide responsibility. Educators and parents must be prepared to meet the challenges of the transitional period from middle school to high school.

The National School Safety Center (1998) offers the following checklist of characteristics of youth that have caused school-associated violent deaths. While this represents extreme data, derived from tracking school-associated violent deaths in the United States, there are some common characteristics of youngsters that indicate their potential for harming themselves or others. These characteristics should serve to alert school administrators, teachers, and support staff to address the needs of troubled students through meetings with parents, the provisions of school counseling, and mentoring services. The profile of an adolescent who has caused a school-related violent death (1998):

1. Has a history of tantrums and uncontrollable angry outbursts;

2. Characteristically resorts to name-calling, cursing, or abusive language;

3. Habitually makes violent threats when angry;

4. Has previously brought a weapon to school;.

5. Has a background of serious disciplinary problems at school and in the community;

6. Has a background of drug, alcohol, or other substance abuse or dependency;

7. Is on the fringe of his/her peer group with few or no close friends;

8. Is preoccupied with weapons, explosives, or other incendiary devices;

9. Has previously been truant, suspended or expelled from school;

10. Displays cruelty to animals;

11. Has little or no supervision and support from parents or a caring adult;

12. Has witnessed or been a victim of abuse or neglect in the home;

13. Has been bullied and/or bullies or intimidates peers or younger children;

14. Tends to blame others for difficulties and problems he/she causes;

15. Consistently prefers TV shows, movies, or music expressing violent themes and acts;

16. Prefers reading materials dealing with violent theme, rituals, and abuse;

17. Reflects anger, frustration, and the dark side of life in essays or writing projects;

18. Is involved with a gang or an antisocial group on the fringe of peer acceptance;

19. Is often depressed and/or has significant mood swings; and

20. Has threatened or attempted suicide.

In all facets of life, transitions are handled more successfully when there are programs in place to help those involved. Mentoring programs are now in place to help new teachers more readily adjust to the classroom environment. Principal mentor programs are in place to aid in the adjustment to the role of administrator. Teenagers who are undergoing a time of complex social adjustment especially need assistance in the transition from middle school to high school. Effective programs can help youth adapt more easily to the unfamiliar high school environment. Successful programs involve strong communication, parental involvement, effective curriculum practices, and a safe, personalized atmosphere. As Lawrence Mayer, principal of Ardsley High School, said, "One of the most crucial rites of passage is the transition from middle to high school. Careful attention to the academic, psychological, social, and emotional needs of students through a planned transition program will help incoming freshmen enter their new world more easily" (1995). School personnel should develop a transition program that would best meet the needs of their students, implement it, continuously assess the program's effectiveness and search for ways to improve.

12

Games and Activities
for Students

Middle school students want to know what high school is going to be like, and they and their parents need to know about and understand high school programs and procedures (Phelan, Yu, and Davidson 1994). Some of the ways students can learn about high school include visiting the high school in the spring, perhaps to "shadow" a high school student; attending a presentation by a high school student or panel of students; visiting the high school in the fall for schedule information; attending a fall orientation assembly (preferably before school starts); and discussing high school regulations and procedures with eighth-grade teachers and counselors. Another possible source of information is the Internet. High school students might set up a Web page that would provide incoming students information on different high school activities and clubs and offer them an opportunity to get answers to any question they may have from the "experts."

At a time when friendships and social interaction are particularly important for young adolescents, the normative transition into high school often serves to disrupt friendship networks and, thereby, interferes with students' success in high school. Thus, it is vital for a transition program to include activities that will provide incoming students social support activities that give students the opportunity to get to know and develop positive relationships with older students and other incoming students. A "Big Sister/Brother" Program that begins in eighth grade and continues through ninth grade, a spring social event for current and incoming high school students, and writing programs where eighth-graders correspond with high school students by letter or e-mail are just a few ways that transition programs can provide students social support. Middle and high school educators should also develop more long-term activities such as peer mentoring or tutoring programs.

Student Games and Activities

Title: The Name Game
Objective: To allow new students to get to know their classmates
Materials: None needed

Procedure: Students gather in a circle. The first person says his/her name. The person to the right says his/her name, plus the name of the previous person. The next person follows the pattern by saying his/her name plus the names of the previous two people. The game continues around the circle until everyone has had a chance to introduce him or herself. The last person in the circle has the challenge of remembering everyone's name.

Title: May I Present
Objective: To allow new students to get to know their classmates
Materials: Paper and pen for each student; suggested list of interview questions, either provided by the teacher or brainstormed by the class

Procedure: Students are assigned a partner. Students spend two to three minutes interviewing each other. When all pairs have interviewed each other, the group reassembles. Each student has an opportunity to introduce his/her partner to the group.

Title: I'd Walk a Million Miles for....
Objective: To allow new students to get to know their classmates
Materials: None needed

Procedure: Students gather in a circle. Each student is given an opportunity to complete this sentence aloud: "I would walk a mile for (or to)..."

Title: We Have So Much in Common
Objective: To allow new students to get to know their classmates and to realize that students have more in common than perhaps they thought.
Materials: Work sheet, pencil or pen

Procedure: Each student finds a partner. Each writes the name of the partner in the first section of the worksheet. The students have two to three minutes to find out the things they have in common, and jot those things on the list. After the allotted time, students find a new partner and repeat the process. The activity is repeated with a third and final partner. After the activity is completed the teacher leads a discussion on the activity. Possible questions are:

- How many things did you find in common?

- What kinds of things did you have in common with your classmates?

- How did you find out these commonalities?

- What do these things tell us about our group?

Title: The Jigsaw Puzzle
Objective: To allow new students to get to know their classmates and to understand that each person brings unique gifts and talents to the group
Materials: Colored pencils, markers, and/or crayons, and teacher pre-pared puzzle pieces. To make these take a piece of poster board or other large study paper and draw puzzle shapes. Make certain there is enough for each student and teacher. Lightly number each piece in the lower right hand corner. Cut out the shapes. Give each student one piece, instructing them draw on the side with the number, but not to cover over the number. This is essential for reassembling the puzzle.

Procedure: Using words and pictures students design their section to illustrate their strengths and talents. Students are provided with an opportunity to discuss their individual puzzle piece. Through discussion the teacher helps the students to understand that the class puzzle is made up of many unique pieces. The puzzle is assembled and displayed.

Things We Have in Common Worksheet

Name _____

1
2
3
4
5
6
7
8
9
10
11
12
13
14
15
16
17
18
19
20

Name _____

1
2
3
4
5
6
7
8
9
10
11
12
13
14
15
16
17
18
19
20

Name _____

1
2
3
4
5
6
7
8
9
10
11
12
13
14
15
16
17
18
19
20

Title: Everyone Loves A Compliment
Objective: To recognize the positive qualities in others, to graciously give and receive compliments, to build self-esteem
Materials: None needed

Procedure: Students and teacher gather in a circle. The teacher introduces the format for giving a compliment, "I would like to compliment (name) for_____." Students are reminded to acknowledge the compliment with, "Thank you." Students compliment the person to their right. The activity continues until all students have given and received a compliment. If this activity is repeated often, the teacher may choose to vary the method. Students may draw a name from a hat and compliment that person, or students may self select who they would like to compliment.

Title: I Was, But Now I Am
Objective: To allow new students to get to know their classmates and to understand that people grow and change.
Materials: None needed

Procedure: Students gather in a circle. Each student is provided with the opportunity to complete this statement: "I used to be_____, but now I am _____." Through discussion the teacher helps the students realize that everyone changes, grows and matures.

Title: Freshman Facts Scavenger Hunt
Objective: To discover information about their new school.

Procedure: Students are grouped in pairs and permitted to use the school/system's code for student conduct and procedure. Interviews with older students or teachers may be used as well.
Materials: Pencil and paper, student handbook, and safe school plan.

1. Who is the principal and who are the assistant principals of your school?

2. If I am late for school in the morning, where do I report?

3. If I am absent from school, what do I need to do when I return to school?

4. If I get ill at school and must go home, what do I do?

5. Where is "Lost and Found"?

6. What is the school mascot? What are the school colors?

7. Will I have a locker? Where will my locker be located and how often may I go to my locker? Can I keep my book bag with me?

8. Can my locker be searched?

9. What can I keep in my locker?

10. If I must leave the room during class, what must I do?

11. Does my school have a student dress code? If so, what is it?

12. Who is the school's resource officer? What is his/her role?

13. If I lose or damage a textbook, what should I do?

14. If I must take medicine, what do I do?

15. How do I see a guidance counselor?

16. Can I get in trouble at school for misbehaving on the bus?

17. Who is the school secretary?

18. What will happen if I am late for a class?

19. What time does school begin and end?

20. What are the procedures in the cafeteria for buying lunch, cleaning up, etc.?

21. Is there a safe school plan? What is included?

Title: Team Building

Objective: To work as a team to accomplish a task without talking.

Procedure: Create two objects with pipe cleaners, Object A and Object B. Place each one in a shoebox. Divide the class into two groups, Team A and Team B. Arrange these teams so that each object is hidden from the opposite team.

Instruct each team to write directions for making the object in your team's box, without talking.

Set a time limit.

Instruct the teams to exchange directions with the other team.

Give each person an envelope with materials needed to make the object.

Instruct each student to make the object according to the other team's directions.

Variations: Use materials such as straws and string, tinker toys, legos, etc. You can also make the objects in teams rather than as individuals. Directions can be provided orally.

Title: Characteristics of Good Listeners
Objective: To help students understand the characteristics of a good listener.
Materials: Attentive Listening Handout

Procedure:

1. Ask students: When you are talking to a person, what do they do to let you know they are listening? Not listening? List and discuss.

2. Say: Being an attentive listener is a very difficult task. It takes the total concentration and focus of the listener. We all listen, but we do not all practice attentive listening. An Attentive listener has three main behaviors: comfortable eye contact, positive body language, and verbal following.

3. Divide the class into three groups. Give each group one behavior to discuss and describe. You may even assign them a role play with the behavior. Allow five to ten minutes.

4. Each group then reports to the rest of the class. Clarify their response with the following information:

   a. Comfortable eye contact—The listener does not stare at the talker, nor does he stare into space.

   b. Positive body language—The listener is aware of his own body language; leaning forward, nodding, etc., rather than turned sideways, working on something else.

   c. Verbal following—Occasionally the listener will stop the talker and clarify, summarize, or restate what the talker is saying.

Closure:

Reflect on the following with the students:

What attentive listening skill is the hardest for you?

What on skill would you like to improve on?

Why would we want to be attentive listeners?

Title: Speaking , Listening, and Observing
Objective: To help students practice good listening.
Materials: None

Procedure:

1. Divide students into triads. Assign parts: Person A is speaker, Person B is listener, Person C is observer. A and B will discuss topic and C will observe. C's role is to be sure that B cannot respond to A until B summarizes what A has said. Once B summarizes and responds to A, then A must summarize before responding to B. After 5-10 minutes, switch roles.

2. Suggested topics:

Dress code

Amount of money made by professional athletes

Should you turn in a friend who has broken the law?

Note: A and B should take opposite points of view.

Closure:

Ask students to reflect on:

Was it difficult to summarize before speaking? Why?

Who do you wish you could teach this to?

13

Games and Activities for Teachers for Staff Development

Underlying successful high-school transition programs are activities that bring middle-school and high-school administrators, counselors, and teachers together to learn about the programs, courses, curriculum, and requirements of their respective schools (Hertzog et al. 1996). Activities that create a mutual understanding of curriculum requirements at both levels and of the young adolescent learner will help educators at both levels to develop a high school transition program to meet the particular needs of their students. In addition to the more typical committee or team meetings with representatives from each level, these activities may include K-12 curriculum planning meetings, and teacher or administrator visitations, observations, and teaching exchanges. Parent involvement in the transition process to high school can be encouraged through a variety of activities. Parents may be invited to participate in a conference (preferably in the middle school) with their child and the high school counselor to discuss course work and schedules, visit the high school with their child in the spring or in the fall, spend a day at the high school to help them understand what their child's life will be like, and help design and facilitate some of the articulation activities for students. In planning activities for parents, high school educators should involve parents of students who are already in high school are an excellent resource for other parents and may also help to encourage new parents to be more involved in school activities. At the middle school level, teachers and administrators can inform parents about transition activities and encourage them to participate. They can work to keep parents involved in their child's education and school activities during the middle school years to that they are comfortable coming to school and confident that their involvement makes a difference in their child's academic success.

Games for Teachers and Staff Development

Title: Teamwork Matters
Target Audience: Teachers
Objective: To help teachers realize that working in teams can accomplish a task more effectively.
Materials: Table or tray with 15-20 assorted objects (book, cup, pencil, magazine…)

Procedure: Teachers position themselves where they can clearly see all the objects. Allow one minute to view the objects. Give teachers one minute to write down as many objects as they can as they can remember. Then group the teachers into several small groups and allow them two minutes to complete a group list. Through discussion compare the easy of the individual task with that of the group. Compare the accuracy of the individual lists as compared to the group lists.

Title: Instructional Scavenger Hunt
Target Audience: Teachers
Objective: To allow teachers to analyze the extent to which different instructional strategies are being used.
Materials: Teacher lesson plans implemented to date, list of instructional strategies

Procedure: Divide the teachers into two or more teams; this may be done by grade level, units, cross grade groups, random groups or other configurations. Provide each group with a list of instructional strategies. Have them find as many lessons as possible that illustrate a particular teaching method.

Title: Teaching Attending Behavior
Goal: To develop several activities that can be used to teach active listening skills to students.

Procedure: In teaching teams, develop activities for teaching active listening to students.
Begin with the Guidelines listed below, but additional guidelines may be added.

Guidelines for Active Listening:

1. Focus on the person who is talking.

   • Maintain a comfortable amount of eye contact.

   • Block out interfering noises, movement, words, and own self-centered thoughts.

2. Be aware of the feelings of the talker.

   • Attempt to listen to more than just the spoken words.

   • Attempt to understand the whole message.

   • Empathize; try to see the world through the eyes of another person.

3. Show that you understand what is being said.

   • Say something that will indicate that you are following the conversation.

   • Periodically check out what you think you are hearing.

   • Try to respond accurately and sensitively to what people say to you.

4. Be a selective listener.

   • Sort out the critical aspects of what is being said.

- Clarify the main issues.

- Stay on task.

5. <u>Avoid labeling or judging the talker</u>.

  - Focus on the personal meaning that the talker gives to the spoken word.

  - Be a caring listener

Title: Team Building for Leadership
Goal: To strengthen team building and leadership skills between the ninth grade teachers.

Procedures: Select from the list of activities:

High/Low Ropes Course

Obstacle Course

Rappelling

Trust Fall

Hula Hoop Pass

Scavenger Hunt

RESOURCES:

Local School ROTC Program
County Ropes Course
School Ropes Course

FOLLOW-UP ACTIVITIES:

Team debriefing
Written reflection
Application to classroom

Appendix A

Queen's Twelve Factors for Successful Transitions

Factor One

The lower the student's grades drop during ninth grade transition, the higher the students' probability of dropping out of school.

(Roderick 1993; Newman, Barbara M; Lohman, Brenda J; Newman, Phillip R; Myers, Mary C.; Smith, Victoria L. 2000; Owing and Peng 1992)

Factor Two

Students who fail during the transition and drop out of school experience lifelong difficulties physically, socially, emotionally, and economically. (Juvonen and Wentzel 1996; Owings and Peng 1992)

Major Study

Newman, Barbara M; Lohman, Brenda J; Newman, Phillip R; Myers, Mary C.; Smith, Victoria L. (2000, June). Experiences of Urban Youth Navigating the Transition to Ninth Grade. *Youth and Society. (31), (4),* 387–417.

The purpose of the authors in this study was to associate factors related to academic success and the coping of low-income, urban, minority adolescents in transition from the eighth to ninth grade. This study assumes that success in high school is directly related to success in college and that since low-income urban students have a low graduation rate from college it is important to examine how these students coped with the transition to high school.

The researchers addressed four major questions:

1. What are the relevant microsystems that affect adolescents' motivation and academic performance in the transition from eighth grade to ninth grade?

2. What are the key elements of those systems that either help sustain or detract from academic motivation and performance?

3. What factors differentiate students who are performing well in ninth grade from those who are having academic difficulties?

4. What strategies do students use to cope with the new and competing demands across settings that accompany the transition to high school?

This author acknowledged the previous research of Eccles, Lord and Buchanan in 1996 as well as that of Simmons and Blythe in 1987 which stated that "theoretical models that attempt to account for students' adaptations to high school typically do not consider concurrent changes in the students' relationships with their peers, family, and neighborhood during the transition to ninth grade." With this in mind it is also noted that previous research has found the negative outcomes of the transition to high school to include the following: "(a) poorer attendance (Barone, Aguirre-Deandreis, and Trickett 1991; Felner, Primavera, and Cauce 1981; Moyer and Motta 1982; Weldy 1990); (b) decline in GPA (Barone et al. 1991; Blyth; Simmons, and Carlton-Ford 1983; Felner, Primavera, and Cauce 1981); (c) Discipline problems associated with experiencing change to a new school building, moving from self-contained to departmentalized classes, or encountering a different educational philosophy (Moyer and Motta 1982; Weldy 1990) and (d) decreased participation in extracurricular activities (Blythe et al. 1983)."

It was noted that there is a direct correlation between students who have success gaining acceptance socially in a new school environment experienced smoother transition than those who do not (Schmidt 1993; Kulka, Kahle, and Klingel 1982). A student's feelings of belongingness are also associated with success in school (Felner, Ginter, and Primavera, 1982; Goodenow 1993). In short, there are many factors that contribute to either the success or failure of students in transition, not only the factors mentioned above but developmental factors as well.

This study involved 29 YSP students, 12 of which had completed the eighth grade and 17 of which had completed the ninth grade. YSP is a program sponsored by Ohio State University and is an early intervention program. Students are nominated at the end of their sixth grade year by members of their community, teachers or parents to be selected for YSP. They must be a member of a low-income family as well as one of the minority groups in Ohio that are underrepresented in the college population. Admittance is based on the nomination as well as academic performance, potential for academic success, leadership, and other talents or abilities. The students attend a three-week summer session every summer until their first year in college (6 sessions). Information was gathered through interviews that were pretested for clarity of question, length, and coverage of issues. Case narratives were developed for each student using tape-recorded interviews, self-report measures of academic self concept (Brookover, Erickson, and Joiner 1967) grades, and information gathered to determine the structure of the school the student was enrolled in.

The findings were multi-faceted.

1. Students felt that difficulty of homework, amount of homework, amount of required study time, increases in expected responsibility, and amount of note-taking required all contributed to making high school more difficult than middle school.

2. The quality of students' relationships with their teachers was important to the students. Common negative comments about teachers included (mentioned by sixteen students): less homework enforcement, bad attitudes, less helpful, more difficult, less supportive, and less time with teachers. Nine students (mentioned common positive comments): good attitudes, good teaching method, more open, more supportive, more helpful.

3. Adjustment to the new school was listed as another point of difficulty for these students. Particular descriptors were: bigger school, new environment, classes involve more participation, class length, and smaller classes.

4. Social adjustment was also a concern. Meeting new people, more friends in classes, being treated more maturely, more conflict and fighting between students.

5. Low performing students commonly mentioned four categories not mentioned by high performing students. These responses or concerns were: ninth grade is easier than eighth grade, smaller classes, involving participation in class, and more fighting.

6. All students felt that they faced challenges in the following microsystems: family, school, peers, and neighborhood.

7. Four major sources were identified as follows: family members, teachers and counselors, peers, and other individuals. Mothers were listed as the primary source of support in academics by 72 percent of the participants.

8. There was no real correlation drawn between the number of support people and academic performance. Low performing students did, however, depend less on family members and more on teachers than high performing students.

9. Students reported three strategies for success. They were individual, academic, and social. The individual strategies were: hard work, dedication, determination, focus, prioritizing, self-discipline, surviving on your own, using time wisely, and trying your best. Academic strategies were: good behavior, doing work, students-teacher cooperation, studying, studying over the summer, and paying attention. Social keys to success were: hanging with the right crowd, encouragement from parents, and belonging to clubs. These keys to social success were all found to help cope with the main social strategy for success that was to resist negative peer pressure.

10. High performing students and low performing students both described high school transition in similar terms. The difference

came in the methods of dealing with difficulty. Lower-level students were less likely to reach out and had smaller support groups than higher-level students.

The students involved in this study felt that teachers were not as helpful as they may have been in middle school and do not seem to monitor students' work as closely. This leads many of them to conclude that teachers do not care about them. This results in decreased motivation and attendance. These students also felt that the challenges of transition could be broken into four basic categories: relationships with teachers, academic difficulties, adjusting to the school environment, and peer or social pressure. The researchers and students concluded that if intervention programs are to be set into place and are to be successful, students should be involved as informed experts about the challenges that they face. Programs must be designed that are adapted to the wide range of problems and challenges students' face.

Students also indicated the family as a strong source of support. "Efforts to support a more successful transition to high school need to include ways of informing family members about the challenges and demands of the high school curriculum and identifying strategies that will strengthen their ability to guide their children's academic success." As far as peers were concerned students felt that the challenge was allocating the right amount of energy and time to peer interactions.

This study concluded that transition to high school is a major stressor in the lives of young people. This stress combined with those associated with maturation and growth combine to create more stress. Students without support have more difficulty with this transition than those with support. The students say that teachers really matter. More ways of enhancing students-teacher relationships must be examined in order to determine ways of making this transition easier on students. The findings of the study also confirm that the family plays a key role in supporting academic achievement in school

Another conclusion of this study was that if achievement is to improve, schools must be sure that every student has at least one adult who is "committed to his or her academic success." The study identified at least three groups of low performing students:

1. Students who are truly alienated from school and have withdrawn their energy from the process.

2. Students who are facing serious challenges, such as family conflicts, the absence of family involvement, courses that are really too hard, and shyness or social rejection, that make the first year of school very difficult.

3. Students who get caught up in the social excitement of high school, and do not have the discipline or motivation to remain focused on their studies.

Schools must intervene and identify students who are in trouble before the end of the ninth grade. They must then invent opportunities for these students to learn from their experiences and make a fresh start.

Alspaugh, John W. (1998, September/October). The achievement loss associated with the transition to middle school and high school. *Journal of Educational Research, 92,* 1, 21–26.

The researcher in this major study explored "the nature of the achievement loss associated with school to school transitions from elementary school to middle school and to high school." A statistically significant achievement loss was found with the transition from elementary school to middle school at the sixth grade level as compared to a K-8 program. Both K-8 and middle school students experienced achievement loss in the transition to ninth grade, however the middle school students experienced a greater loss than the K-8 students did. The high school dropout rates were also higher for middle school students than for the K-8 students.

This study sights the following changes associated with the transition to high school:

1. Elementary school goals tend to be task oriented while middle schools focus on performance (Midgley, Anderman, and Hicks 1995).

2. Student-teacher relationships change from elementary school to middle school (Midgley, Feldlaufer, and Eccles 1988).

3. The change from small-group and individual instruction to whole-class instruction in middle school.

4. Researchers have found declines in student self-perception and self-esteem associated with the transition from elementary to the intermediate level (Seidman, Allen, Abet, Mitchell, and Feinmann 1994; Wigfield, Eccles, Mac Iver, Reuman, and Midgley 1991). Siedman et al. found the decline tin self-perception to be independent of age, grade level, and ability level.

In 1995 Alspaugh and Hatting found that there is acheivement loss in the transition from elementary to middle school, but that acheivement scores tend to recover the year following the transition.

The sample consisted of three groups of 16 school districts for a total of 48 districts. One group had only one high school and one elementary school. The second group had one elementary school, one middle school and one high school. The third group had two or three elementary schools, one middle school and one high school. The K-8 group experienced gains in test scores while the other two groups, which transitioned to middle schools, experienced achievement loss. The achievement loss in the third group, the group that drew from more than one elementary school, was greater than that of the group that drew from only one elementary school. The achievement loss in the transition to high school was significant in all three groups. However, the achievement loss in the third group was greater than in the second group and the achievement loss for the K-8 group was less than either group two or group three.

A statistical significance was found between the dropout rates in the K-8 school and the dropout rates in the two groups from the middle schools. There were two transitions for the middle school groups and only one transition for the K-8 group. "This finding implies that the students were encountering a double-jeopardy situation that Seidman et al. (1994) anticipated." Seidman hypothesized that students who make two transitions have more difficulty and higher dropout rates that those who do not (1994).

The researcher concluded that students who are placed in "relatively small cohort groups for long spans of time tend to experience more desirable educational outcomes."

Southern Regional Education Board. (2001, Summer). Transition program. Summer Bulletin.

The researchers begin this bulletin by describing briefly the problems associated with the transition to the ninth grade. The researchers list the following as problems associated with the transition:

- Low attendance levels
- Higher number of tardies
- The highest percentage of failing grades
- The highest percentage of over-aged students
- The highest suspension rate

The main factor that the researchers identified for the difficulties associated with transition is a failure on the part of the middle schools to academically prepare the students for high school and the failure of the high school to allow for the students to make the transition.

The researchers suggested that middle schools increase the intensity and quality of their curriculum, that high schools increase the intensity and quality of their curriculum, that middle schools and high schools work together through vertical teaming to create a solid cohesive curriculum, establishing and maintaining a flexible scheduling and curriculum patterns to provide structure and stability, and that high schools and middle schools should work together to develop structured transition programs.

Neild, Ruth; Stoner-Eby, Scott; Furstenberg, Frank Jr.; (2001, January 13) *Connecting entrance and departure: The transition to ninth grade and high school dropout.* **Paper presented at Dropouts in America, Harvard University.**

The author of this paper described the dropout rates of Philadelphia schools, citing the Philadelphia Education Longitudinal Study as the source of data. This data suggests that failing ninth grade substantially increases the chances of dropping out of high school. Other significant factors that contributed to increased dropout rates were if students were male, older, hang with a bad crowd, and were less academically engaged in school as eighth graders.

Students who were more involved academically in ninth grade, who were more interested in their classes, and were not bored were less likely to dropout. Factors that increase student achievement and completion included higher quality, more engaging teachers, and higher comfort levels and feelings of safety among students.

The findings suggested that students who are having trouble or are failing the eighth grade should be given extra help and attention, citing double-blocking, cohort groups, and separate ninth grade centers as strategies for success. Using these methods promotion rates increased by 47 percent in one school, and 65 percent in another. Decreases in behavior problems, suspensions, and hallway disturbances were observed as well.

The authors call for radical changes in the framework of modern high schools, including revisiting the notion of K-12 schools.

Factor Three

The larger the high school, the greater the negative impact of transition on ninth grade students.

(Balfanz and Legters 2001; Ancess and Wichterle 2001; Oxley, Croninger, and DeGroot 2000

Alspaugh, John W. (1998, March) The relationship of school-to-school transitions and school size to dropout rates. *High School Journal*, (3), 154–160.

Southern Regional Education Board. (2001, Summer). Transition program. Summer Bulletin.

Neild, Ruth; Stoner-Eby, Scott; Furstenberg, Frank Jr.; (2001, January 13) *Connecting entrance and departure: The transition to ninth grade and high school dropout.* Paper presented at Dropouts in America, Harvard University.

Fox, Joanna. (2000, July). *Getting ninth graders ready to succeed in high school. Resource Packet.* **Paper presented at High Schools That Work. Summer Conference, Nashville, TN.**

Recommendations for the improvement of the ninth grade system were based on the research of the Southern Regional Education Board and included the following:

- Focus on curriculum and instruction
- Double-blocking of core classes in weak areas
- Teaching reading and critical thinking skills
- Algebra I
- Inquiry and lab-based sciences
- Career awareness programs
- Guidance, advisement, and parent participation
- Vertical teaming
- Use and space of facilities
- Professional development
- Orient parents and students to high school
- More personal attention, improved teacher-student relationships
- Smallness-violence and at-risk behaviors reduced, attendance and motivation increase
- Use of data to analyze the impact of interventions and policies and the modification of strategies as indicated.

Mizelle, Nancy B.; Irvin, Judith L.; *Transtion from middle school into high school.* **Captured from www.nmsa.org/services/ transition.htm on 1/8/02.**

The researchers conclude that it is time to "reemphasize articulation as a function of middle level education." More time needs to be spent helping middle school students become better prepared for high school to ease the transition. The researchers also call for vertical teaming and more cooperation between teachers involved at all levels: elementary, middle, and high school. It is also stated that as young people enter the high school they experience differences in teachers, teaching styles, peer involvement, more responsibility, and a more impersonal, competitive environment. If the transition is not a smooth one, many students experience a drop in grades, drop in attendance, and they may begin to develop a more negative attitude about themselves and school. Some of the fears of transition students that are listed by the researchers are: a fear of being teased, getting lost, failing, and that the teachers are more strict and do not care as much. The researchers recommend that transition programs provide the students and parents with information about high school, provide students with social support, and include vertical teaming and cooperation between the sending and receiving schools.

Factor Four

Students once in school and, experience two or more transitions prior to ninth grade have a greater probability of quitting high school. (Wood 1993)

Newman, Barbara M; Lohman, Brenda J; Newman, Phillip R; Myers, Mary C.; Smith, Victoria L. (2000, June). Experiences of Urban Youth Navigating the Transition to Ninth Grade. *Youth and Society. (31)*, (4), 387–417.

Alspaugh, John W. (1998, September/October). The achievement loss associated with the transition to middle school and high school. *Journal of Educational Research, 92,* 1, 21–26.

Alspaugh, John W. (1998, March) The relationship of school-to-school transitions and school size to dropout rates. *High School Journal,* (3), 154–160.

Southern Regional Education Board. (2001, Summer). Transition program. Summer Bulletin.

Factor Five

High school dropout rates are higher for middle school students than for students attending K-8 schools. (Mizelle, 1999).

Alspaugh, John W. (1998, March) The relationship of school-to-school transitions and school size to dropout rates. *High School Journal*, (3), 154–160.

Alspaugh, John W. (1998, September/October). The achievement loss associated with the transition to middle school and high school. *Journal of Educational Research, 92*, 1, 21–26

Neild, Ruth; Stoner-Eby, Scott; Furstenberg, Frank Jr.; (2001, January 13) *Connecting entrance and departure: The transition to ninth grade and high school dropout.* Paper presented at Dropouts in America, Harvard University.

Factor Six

Ninth grade student's adjustment to high school is complicated by their perceptions of a bigger school, different environment, changed class schedule, and by smaller classes.
(Reyes, Gillock, Kobus, and Sanchez 2000; Ancess and Wichterle 2001; Legters 2000, Bank Street College "Small Schools, Great Strides" 2001; Johnson 2002; Hampel 2002)

Newman, Barbara M; Lohman, Brenda J; Newman, Phillip R; Myers, Mary C.; Smith, Victoria L. (2000, June). Experiences of Urban Youth Navigating the Transition to Ninth Grade. *Youth and Society. (31)*, (4), 387–417.

Alspaugh, John W. (1998, September/October). The achievement loss associated with the transition to middle school and high school. *Journal of Educational Research, 92*, 1, 21–26.

Neild, Ruth; Stoner-Eby, Scott; Furstenberg, Frank Jr.; (2001, January 13) *Connecting entrance and departure: The transition to ninth grade and high school dropout.* Paper presented at Dropouts in America, Harvard University.

Mizelle, Nancy B.; Irvin, Judith L.; *Transtion from middle school into high school.* Captured from www.nmsa.org/services/transition.htm on 1/8/02.

Factor Seven

Fear of getting lost in the high school building is by far the number one fear of ninth grade students. (Capelluti and Stokes 1991; Rossi and Stokes 1991; Davis 1998; Queen 2000)

Mizelle, Nancy B.; Irvin, Judith L.; *Transtion from middle school into high school.* Captured from www.nmsa.org/services/transition.htm.

Factor Eight

Ninth-grade students view high school teachers as less helpful than middle school teachers. (Midgley, Eccles, & Feldlaufer, 1991; Murdock, Anderman, & Hodge 2000; Queen 2000)

Newman, Barbara M; Lohman, Brenda J; Newman, Phillip R; Myers, Mary C.; Smith, Victoria L. (2000, June). Experiences of Urban Youth Navigating the Transition to Ninth Grade. *Youth and Society. (31),* (4), 387–417.

Alspaugh, John W. (1998, September/October). The achievement loss associated with the transition to middle school and high school. *Journal of Educational Research, 92,* 1, 21–26.

Southern Regional Education Board. (2001, Summer). Transition program. Summer Bulletin.

Factor Nine

Ninth grade students must have at least one adult in their lives for genuine support in order to become academically and socially successful. (Anderson, Jacobs, Schramm, and Splittgerber 2000)

Newman, Barbara M; Lohman, Brenda J; Newman, Phillip R; Myers, Mary C.; Smith, Victoria L. (2000 June). Experiences of Urban Youth Navigating the Transition to Ninth Grade. *Youth and Society. (31)*, (4), 387–417.

Alspaugh, John W. (1998 September/October). The achievement loss associated with the transition to middle school and high school. *Journal of Educational Research, 92,* 1, 21–26.

Alspaugh, John W. (1998 March) The relationship of school-to-school transitions and school size to dropout rates. *High School Journal,* (3), 154–160.

Southern Regional Education Board. (2001 Summer). Transition program. Summer Bulletin.

Factor Ten

Ninth-grade students who have negative experiences during the transitional period have poor attendance, low grades, and fewer friends. They tend to become behavior problems and have greater vulnerability to negative peer influence.

(Smith 1997; Reyes, Gillock, Kobus, and Sanchez 2000; Anderson, Jacobs, Schramm, and Splittgerber 2000; Loeber and Farrington 1998; Louis Harris and Associates 1998; Queen 2000)

Newman, Barbara M; Lohman, Brenda J; Newman, Phillip R; Myers, Mary C.; Smith, Victoria L. (2000 June). Experiences of Urban Youth Navigating the Transition to Ninth Grade. *Youth and Society. (31)*, (4), 387–417.

Southern Regional Education Board. (2001 Summer). Transition program. Summer Bulletin.

Neild, Ruth; Stoner-Eby, Scott; Furstenberg, Frank Jr.; (2001 January 13) *Connecting entrance and departure: The transition to ninth grade and high school dropout.* Paper presented at Dropouts in America, Harvard University.

Factor Eleven

Dropout rates will increase for poorly transitioned students, especially minority students, in schools using high stakes testing. (Roderick 1993; Hauser 1997; Anyon1999; A National Comparison 2000; NC DPI 2001)

Factor Twelve

Social and economic factors negatively impact graduation rates, especially in large urban areas.

(Robertson 1997; Aronowitz and De Fazio 1997; Neef 1998; Murdock et al. 2000; Phelan, P, Davidson, A. and Cao, H. 1991; Bureau of Labor Statistics 2001; A National Comparison 2000 Census; Casualties of School Reform, Cenzipper 2001)

Belfanz, Robert; Legters, Nettie. (2001, January) *How many central city high schools have a severe dropout problem, where are they located, and who attends them? Estimates using the common core of data.* **Paper presented at Dropouts in America, Harvard University.**

The researchers conclude that in the country's largest 35 central cities, the "urban dropout problem may be concentrated in 200–300 schools." The schools with the weakest "holding power" are large, over 900 students, and have a minority population of 90 percent or more. Drastic reform is needed in cities in which the failure rates are this high in five or more schools, and drastic reform is needed on the individual site level in all other cases. The schools must be turned around. The highest concentration of failing schools is in the industrial northwest and Midwest.

Appendix B

Surveys, Tips, and Related Resources

An Example of One School's Approach in Using Advisor/Advisee Groups

Using advisor/advisee groups, which were called Navigators. In January of 2000 after a semester of research and planning, the faculty came up with this name because we are the Enka Jets—and navigators "help you get to where you want to go."

Structure

In an effort to keep the number in each group as low as possible, every teacher, media coordinator, and administrator was assigned a Navigator group. Our support personnel were also invited to have a group. Even though they were not required to, most of them wanted to have a group. This allowed us to have groups with no more than 16 and upper level groups usually have less. Guidance personnel do not have a group in order to serve as a resource for teachers during the Navigator time. They usually "walk the halls" checking on groups and making sure all students are in class.

Navigator leaders are paired up. We did this for several reasons:

1. If a leader is absent, the groups can be put together and one leader conducts both groups. (This is particularly crucial for administrators—each administrator is paired with a teacher, not

another administrator. Invariably, there are times when the administrator has to be gone.)

2. Promote a feeling of security on the part of the navigator leaders. Some leaders feel more confident in conducting groups than others. At times they may choose to put their groups together, although we do not recommend it all the time.

3. Support personnel are paired with classroom teachers to make use of educational expertise.

We allowed leaders to choose their partner suggesting that, as much as possible, they choose male/female or academic/vocational partnerships. We also knew that some people are naturally more nurturing than others—this could help in a partnership. We encouraged leaders to discuss the lesson plans with their partner or in their department.

Navigator leaders keep their groups for four years in order to get to know the students and their families better. The idea is that a Navigator leader will hopefully see early signs of negative changes that need to be addressed (increased absences, sliding grades, disciplinary actions, possible drug use, etc.) When seniors graduate, a Navigator leader will pick up a freshman group the following year. Because of dropouts (which we are trying to curtail) freshmen groups with around 16 drop to 10 or 12 by the time they are seniors.

Although a Navigator group starts out with one grade level, during the four years the group may become a mixture of grade levels as one or two students fail courses and are not promoted. We decided to keep them in the same group in order to maintain that relationship and provide better service to them. These are often the students who are falling through the cracks and need someone to know them well. A student might "skip" their junior year because they were technically a sophomore twice but then caught back up.

Navigator Committee

We have a Navigator committee that is composed of an administrator, a guidance counselor, and four teachers. This committee sets up the calendar for Navigator meetings for the year and determines the lesson plans. Each of the four teachers on the committee takes charge of a grade level and is responsible for creating the lesson plans and getting them out to the teachers.

Meeting times

Navigator groups meet for 30 minutes every three weeks from 11:10 to 11:40. Since Navigators take the place of homeroom, we also have what is known as "Navigator Briefings" as needed. These are functional homeroom-type meetings for elections or dissemination of information. We do not want the regular Navigator meetings to turn into a glorified homeroom or study hall.

Attendance is taken during first period and we do not meet "homeroom" on a daily basis.

Lesson Plans

Each 30-minute Navigator session has a definite lesson plan for each grade level. We have seven goals our lesson plans address (see attached sheet). We try to alleviate as much stress as possible for Navigator leaders so all material for a lesson is duplicated for them and placed in their box.

After this first year, our lesson plans are fairly well in place and will only require minor revisions. Each year they will be evaluated for changes.

Many of our lessons have been taken from TEAM—Teachers as Educational Advisors and Mentors. This can be purchased for about $20 ordered from:

Louisiana Department of Education
Office of Vocational Education
PO Box 94064
Baton Rouge, Louisiana 70804

This is a wonderful resource—it divides the lessons into five areas: Self-Knowledge, Life Skills, Educational Development, Work Ethics, and Career Planning. Best of all, it even divides activities into grade levels and the activities build on one another.

Career Interests

One of the goals of our Navigator groups is to have our students better prepared for the workplace, which means taking the appropriate courses in high school. This begins with administering *Choices* to the rising freshmen during registration. Also, the freshmen Navigator groups complete a *SDS* (Self-Directed Search) in Navigators to help determine career choices and a pathway.

In an effort to get parents more involved, Navigator leaders set up appointments with parents of students in their group during the week of registration. This improves communication with parents making them aware of new requirements for graduation, career pathways, and opportunities for special programs such as after-school tutoring, dual enrollment courses at the community college, and advanced placement courses. As a result of these efforts, enrollment in honors and advanced level courses have increased.

One of the things we do in our Navigator group prior to registration is to have the students take their transcript and use the "Transcript Analysis" sheet that we created according to the courses we offer. Each of our courses is assigned a career pathway. Students then mark the grade they made in the class and can see "how far they have to go" to complete a pathway. If a student doesn't pass a class, a grade cannot be put down. For some students, the light bulb finally turns on that you can take a class but if you don't pass it, you don't receive credit! It is also an easy thing to look at for a teacher to see what courses have been taken and if they meet requirements for the next level course.

Teacher Buy-In

Are all our teachers in favor of having a Navigator group? Maybe not everyone! But after one year, most teachers definitely see the need and benefits in having advisor/advisee groups. When we were researching advisee programs, one teacher said to us "Even if we do not have 100% buy in, we're definitely doing better than we did before—which was nothing." It's hard to tell who on staff might not be in full support of the program. After receiving very positive comments from the community, staff are either in favor of the program or are keeping their opinions to themselves!

Navigator Pointers

Discipline

Remember that this is a class even if there is not a grade. All discipline rules are in effect and detention should be assigned as appropriate. If you are having trouble with a student:

1. Try talking to the student alone—away from your Navigator group. Perhaps go find him/her during your planning period and appeal to his/her reasonable side. You might be able to discover what is causing the negative behavior and get to know the student better.

2. Assign detention.

3. If the problem still persists, refer the student to an administrator where the possibility of changing groups will be explored.

Transcript Analysis

The tenth and eleventh grades looked at the Transcript Analysis sheet this last time and the ninth will fill them out February 29. Various questions came up. That's great! Both you and the students are gaining a better understanding of the curriculum. Understand that you are really *not supposed* to know everything! Just answer what you can and talk to your partner or members of your department to find out other answers as much as possible.

1. Tell the student to make an appointment with Guidance, particularly if he thinks his transcript is wrong—the counselors will call him/her when they have time. (This is what they're there for!). We have found several "No Credit" due to attendance that have not been changed, but for the most part we've discovered that the transcripts have NOT been wrong—the students just didn't know what they had passed!

2. On the analysis sheet, have the students fill out their grade in the class, not just a check. This will help to see trends and what

a student is ready for without having to go back and look at other sheets.

3. The letters under the Flags column—you really don't need to know this. However, U stands for a course that fulfills University requirements, P is for a course in Progress.

4. Remember—the course doesn't count if the student doesn't receive a passing grade!

5. When trying to determine pathways, some students could have two or more. A student who is college bound could be in Arts and Science AND another pathway.

6. For current ninth graders—each student MUST complete a pathway to graduate. They must either take Algebra II and complete Arts & Science OR fulfill the coursework for one of the other pathways.

Folders

This has been the hard part since we are not working with SIMS but maintaining an individual database for each grade level. Students enter, leave, or move grade levels (like they did after first semester) and it may not get changed on all databases. We are working on this! This should not be a problem next fall when all Navigator groups are listed in SIMS.

1. If you have a folder on a student whom you have never seen and has not been on the absence list, that student may have been switched. Please send the folder to <name> and we will get it to the right group.

2. If you have a student who does NOT have a folder, please let <name> know and we will get it to the right group.

3. If you do not receive a transcript for each student please let <name> know ASAP. The morning of the Navigator group will be too late to do anything!

4. If a student folder is missing the four-year plan, you may pick up extra copies in <name's> office under the Volunteer board.

Many students have made positive comments about the groups. This is a big undertaking and you are doing a good job for a beginning effort. The Navigator concept has the potential to be one of the best things we can do for our students!

Tips for Top Advisors Using an Advisor/Advisee Program

- Allow group time to discuss problems/concerns. It is often good to arrange students in a circle where everyone can see each other. When discussing, you should sit also to put everyone on "equal footing."

- Always have a purpose. Keep expectations realistic-Focus on why we are here. Get to know students as people-Allow student to "gel"—talk individually with them whenever possible.

- Follow the planned agenda/activities—but use your own style always. Students appreciate an agenda/purpose instead of "study time."

- Keep informed of grade level, academic progress, activities, and interests.

- Show genuine interest and student will respond.

- Keep an open mind toward the program and be flexible with your students.

- Don't be slack on discipline just because it's advisement. Use "tough love" if necessary.

- Be prepared for hostility from some students. Because they receive no grade, they may de-value the program. Don't fall into the same trap.

- Know where to go for answers. Kids ask the strangest things! Utilize the guidance counselors—they have a lot of information available.

- Remember, it takes time to make the program successful.

Student Interest Survey

Name:_____Date:_____

Students: Please choose three items from the following list related to your interests and rank the three with a #1 for your choice, a #2 for your second choice and a #3 for your third choice.

_____ You like to produce art, to use your imagination, to think of new ways to do things, to create something out of nothing.

_____ You like to spend time with people, to talk to people, to meet new people, to relate to other people, to participate in group activities.

_____ You like math and science, to define and solve problems, to do puzzles and crosswords, to figure out how things work, to break a problem into more manageable parts, to test things to see if they work.

_____ You like to plan and arrange, to collect things, to put things in order, to put structure into place, to arrange the parts of something so they work as a whole, to develop systems.

_____ You like to guide and direct people, to be in charge, to have people look up to you, to be the captain of a team, to be responsible for people or projects.

_____ You like to listen to people, to help people, to connect with people, to teach, to guide people, to be a role model, to be responsible for people or projects.

_____ You like to fix things, to take things apart and put them back together, to learn how things work by trial and error, to be practical, to solve problems, to use your hands.

_____ You like to convince people through writing or speaking, to help people learn new things, to use language to help other people understand things, to share ideas.

Home email address:_____
Career Objective: _____
Assigned to _____ Date: _____

Survey for Middle/High School Teachers

Safe Schools

1. Are you familiar with the procedures prescribed in your school's "Safe School's Plan"?

   _____ Yes_____ No

2. Did you participate in the development of your "Safe School's Plan"?

   _____ Yes_____ No

3. Do you feel safe, personally, while at school?

   _____ Yes_____ No

4. Have you ever been the victim of a violent act at school (other than verbal abuse?)

   _____ Yes_____ No

5. If yes, please check the type of incident or incidents in which you were involved.

   Physical Attack _____

   Being Threatened and Pushed _____

   Display of Weapons _____

   Robbery _____

   Improper Touching _____

   Vandalism of Personal Property _____

6. Are students safe at your school?

   _____ Yes____ No

7. Have dangerous weapons been confiscated at your school during the past school year?

   _____ Yes____ No

8. Should law enforcement officers be stationed in schools?

_____ Yes ____ No

9. Do teachers need more legal protection against those who harass them?

_____ Yes____ No

10. Is discipline worse in your school than it was five years ago?

_____ Yes____ No

Freshman Committee Transition Survey

Teachers, do you have a freshman "orientation" program? If so,

1. Are there activities in eighth grade to help prepare students for the transition?

2. Are ninth grade activities planned throughout the year as well as at the beginning?

3. Do you have a team approach? If so, how do you address staffing needs? E.g., planning time, number of courses assigned to a teacher, availability of electives, etc. How are teams determined?

4. Is there parental involvement at any level in this process?

5. Are the freshmen academically graded differently from the rest of the student body? Are they housed differently?

6. If you don't team, are there other organizational structures or curriculum changes you have put in place to help students in grade nine be successful?

7. If you have large numbers of ninth grade students not promoted to tenth grade, do you have a program to address this?

8. Do you have a mentor/mentee or advisor/advisee program? If so, how does it work?

9. Do you evaluate the effectiveness of your program? If so, how?

Parade Magazine, September 19, 1999, Listed 13 Tips for Freshmen—from a Senior Class

Their senior class advice was as follows:

Grades are important, but don't let them become your whole life, or you'll be stressed out all the time.

Get a locker near friends—and if upperclassmen are around, don't stroll too close to their lockers.

Don't let other people bring you down—and some will try, especially if you get good grades.

Watch with whom you mess with. Everybody has an older brother.

Don't get into trouble, because it goes on your permanent record.

Teachers say they don't play favorites or give good grades if you kiss up, but they do.

Electives such as phys ed are easy A's. Don't mess up your grade by skipping or by not dressing for gym.

Get involved in after-school activities. They make it easier to get up in the morning.

Don't stay up all night—it's harder to get up in the morning.

Try your best to stay awake in class.

Teachers won't let you turn in late work all the time.

Stay on top of work, because the road to success is even longer than ninth grade.

Make these next four years count. You'll never have another opportunity like this—unless you have to repeat a year.

Parents! Help your Child Survive Freshman Year!

1. Expect your child to GO TO CLASS! Students who show up regularly and turn in homework rarely fail.

2. Students will WORK HARDER in school than in middle school. There is no free lunch-successful students study several hours every day.

3. Students should also PLAY HARD. Research shows that students who participate in school and community events do better in school than those who don't. Involvement in or attending sports, plays, concerts, and clubs makes school more fun. Of course, leading a balanced life is important.

4. While parents cannot select friends for their children, talk about the idea of CHOOSING FRIENDS WISELY as having an impact on who they will become. Winners select winners. Losers select losers.

5. Encourage your child to get help early. Too many students wait until the last minute to try to pass a class. Teachers are on duty during Academic Enhancement time after school daily to give one-to-one help.

6. Student who develop a relationship with an adult mentor (a teacher, counselor, secretary, friend of the family, etc.) are more likely to survive high school.

7. Freshmen are required to keep a calendar/organizer (Planner) of daily homework. Parents should ask to see these planners. In some cases parents may wish to visit with teachers and ask to have daily assignments initialed. Teacher signatures are kept on file in the main office.

8. Ninth graders need to master some basic study skills. Students should ask teachers what skills are useful and appropriate for that individual course. Reading and note-taking methods are taught in several ninth-grade classes, and counselors can assist students with organization and time management skills.

9. Freshmen should begin career planning early. The counseling center has several good tools for this purpose. Students who begin to set career goals tend to have more direction in school and do better overall than those who have no concept of what they will do after high school.

10. Being an explorer of ideas

- Encouraging students

- Helping students explore non-traditional ideas

- Being role models for work habits, handling stress, over-coming obstacles

- Supporting active learning

- Doing subtle planning in the summer (reading, allowing students to make decisions, giving students responsibility, promoting good choices, and communicating with adults)

- Stretch themselves academically

A Sample Model Transition Schedule

THE COUNTDOWN FOR WKHS' CLASS OF 2003

EVENT	LOCATION	DATE	CHECK OFF
Attend Transition/ Registration Meeting	WKHS Auditorium	January 14 7:00 pm	
Curriculum Night	WKHS Auditorium	January 22 7:00 pm	
Complete Parent/ Student Registration Packet	Return to Middle School	Friday January 24	
Students complete Self-Profile and writing sample	In English Class	Wednesday January 22	
Teachers complete Student Profile and make recommendations	Middle Schools	Middle School Principal's Deadline	
Final Registration	Middle School	Monday	

EVENT	LOCATION	DATE	CHECK OFF
Requests and Student Info Packet submitted to WKHS	Send to WKHS	February 10	
Copy of Request sent home	Middle Schools mail to parents	February 17-24	
Registration Teams review materials and assign students to courses	WKHS	February 18, 19	
Clean-up of scan sheets and late registrations	WKHS	Last Week of February	
Course verifications sent home	WKHS mails to parents	March 17-20	
Respond with corrections to Course Verifications	Call or mail to WKHS	By April 1	
Last Day of Classes	Middle Schools	June 6	
Begin summer reading list	Home	June 9	
Get Physical exam for athletes; submit record	Return to WKHS	Before July 30	
Freshman Schedule Pick-up	WKHS	August 12	
Complete summer reading	Home	August 15	
First Day of Classes 2002-2002 (Freshmen only)		August 16	

Source: American Secondary Education, Vol. 26, No. 1

Sample High School Letter to Parents of Eighth Grade Students

March 2, 2002

Name
Address
City, State ZIP

Dear _____

SUBJECT: Registration Conference for _____

Parent/teacher conferences for the rising freshmen will take place at <name> High School in the Media Center on March 21 and 23 from 4:00 pm through 8:00 pm. Your scheduled time is xxx.

If this is not a convenient time, please send me alternative dates and times on the enclosed response card by March 15. Or you can call <name> in the Guidance Office to reschedule a more convenient time.

This conference is an opportunity for us to meet and complete the registration of your child for the 2000-01 school year. Please bring the registration card that <name> will receive on March 20 at <name> Middle School. We request that you arrive 10-15 minutes before your appointment so <name> will have time to complete a computerized career interest survey. This information will be used in the conference.

You are always welcome to request additional conference at any time. Our time together during this conference will help us build our partnership in your child's education. We look forward to meeting with you.

Sincerely,

<Name>, Chairman
Freshmen Parent/Teacher Conference Committee

Enclosure

Ninth Grade Team Interest and Intent Form

Teachers interested in participating in the Ninth Grade Team should submit this complete form to the principal by _____
Teacher's Name: _____   Date: _____

1. Please place a check beside the your preference of a schedule.
    _____ 1 block of 90 minutes each semester with three traditional yearlong classes
    _____ 2 blocks of 90 minutes each with two traditional yearlong classes
    _____ 3 blocks of 90minutes each semester with a 95 minute planning period

2. Place a check beside all the classes that you would be willing to teach.
    _____ English I   _____ Honors English I
    _____ Introduction to Math   _____ Algebra I
    _____ Geometry   _____ World Studies
    _____ ELPS   _____ Earth/Env. Science
    _____ Physical Science   _____ Biology

3. Are you willing to attend the necessary staff development activities specifically designed for ninth grade teachers?

                    Yes   No

4. What characteristics do you possess that will be beneficial to the Team?

5. Briefly state why you are interested in participating on a ninth grade team.

How to Improve Parent Conference Registration

Parent Involvement—Rising Freshmen

Question: How can we change the registration process to include a career interest survey, involve the parents, and help our students choose appropriate electives?

One Possible Solution: Change the registration process to include a computerized career interest inventory and invite parents to the high school for a conference during the week of registration.

- Database of rising freshmen, parents' names and addresses, and appointment times

- Mail merge a letter to parents of each student with a scheduled appointment time between 4:00–8:00 p.m. on one of two evenings in March (example attached)

- Upon arrival, student is directed to computer lab to complete a short career interest survey.

- Student and parents then meet with one of the faculty members to discuss the results the survey and discuss the registration card.

- Other information related to the beginning of the school year can be discussed.

- Advisor/advisee program is explained

What are other solutions?

1.

2.

3.

References

Allan, J., & McKean, J. (1984). Transition to junior high school: Strategies for change. *School Counselor, 32*(1), 43–48.

Allstate Insurance, A. (2001). *Safer schools: Strategies for educators and law enforcement to prevent violence.*

Alspaugh, J. (1998). Achievement loss associated with the transition to middle school and high school. *The Journal of Educational Research, 92*(1), 20–25.

Alspaugh, John W. (1998, March) The relationship of school-to-school transitions and school size to dropout rates. *High School Journal,* (3), 154–160.

Alspaugh, John W. (1998, September/October). The achievement loss associated with the transition to middle school and high school. *Journal of Educational Research, 92,* 1, 21–26.

Anderson, L.W., Jacobs, J., Schramm, S., Splittgerber, F. (2000). School transitions: Beginning or the end of a new beginning? *International Journal of Educational Research, 33*(4), 326–336.

Anyon, J. (1997). *Ghetto schooling: A political economy of urban educational reform.* NY: Teachers College Press.

Archer, J. (2001). New roles tap expertise of teachers. *Education Week.,* Retrieved from the World Wide Web, July 21, 2001.

Aronowitz, S., and Fazio, W. (1997). The new knowledge work. In A. H. Halsey and H. Lauder and P. Brown and A. S. Well (Eds.), *Education: culture, economy, society.* NY: Oxford University Press.

Arsenio, W., Cooperman, S., and Lover, A. (2000). Affective predictors of preschoolers' aggression and peer acceptance direct and indirect effects. *Developmental Psychology, 36*(4), 438–448.

Belfanz, Robert; Legters, Nettie. (2001, January) How many central city high schools have a severe dropout problem, where are they located, and who attends them? Estimates using the common core of data. Paper presented at Dropouts in America, Harvard University.

Berman, S. H. (1998). The bridge to civility: Empathy, ethics, and service. *School Administrator, 55*(5), 27–32.

Bernardo, R., and Neal, J. (1997). In pursuit of the moral school. *Journal of Education, 179*(3), 33–44.

Bloom, B. (1978). Marital disruption as a stressor. In D.G. Forgays (Ed.) *Primary prevention of psychopathy.* (Vol. 2, p. 81–101). Hanover, NH: University Press of New England.

Bracey, G. W. (1994). Dropping in on dropping out. *Phi Delta Kappan, 75*, 726–727.

Brown, P., and Lauder, H. (1997). Education, globalization, and economic development. In A. H. Halsey and H. Lauder and P. Brown and A. S. Wells (Eds.), *Education: culture, economy, society.* NY: Oxford University Press.

Burnham, J.F. (2001). A study of north carolina principal fellows' perceptions of the adequacy of their administrative training. Unpublished Doctoral Dissertation, University of North Carolina at Charlotte.

Caldwell, B.J., Clark, T., Codding, J. B., Eastin, D., Tucker, M.S., and Williams, B. (1999). In D. Marsh (Ed.), *1999 ASCD yearbook: Preparing our schools for the 21st century.* Alexandria, VA: Association for Supervision and Curriculum Development.

Carnegie Corporation Council on Adolescent Development (1996). *Great Transitions: Preparing adolescents for a new century.* New York, NY.

Catterall, J. (1995). Risk and resilience in student transitions to high school. *American Journal of Education, 106*(2), 302–335.

Cresswell, R. (1997). Developing a structure for personalization in the high school. *In the Mood of the American Youth* (Ed.).

DaGiau, B. (n.d.). *A program of counseling and guidance to facilitate the transition form middle school to high school* (ERIC Digest). Montclair, NJ: Montclair NJ.

Daly, J. (1996). Teaching values in everything we do: The nativity experience. *NAASP*, 80. 74–78.

Davis, S. (1998). Personalizing the high school. *Education Week.* Retrieved from the World Wide Web, July 23, 2001.

Dougherty, J.F., Greenspan, N., and Rodahan, M. (1996). SUCCEED with troubled adolescents. *Education Digest, 62*(3), 45–47.

Dugger,W. E. (2001). Standards for technological literacy. *Phi Delta Kappan, 82*(7), 513–517.

Duke, D., & Griesdorn, J. (1999). Considerations in the design of alternative schools. *Clearing House, 73* (2), p. 89–93.

Educational vital signs: Building and bonds. (1994). *The American School Board Journal, 181*(12), A16–A17.

Enrollment boom projected over next ten years. (1997). *National School Board Association, 17*(3), 3.

Espelage, D., Bosworth, K., and Simon, T. (2000). Examining the social context of bullying behaviors in early adolescence. *Journal of Counseling and Development, 78*(3), 326–334.

Ellis, T. (1991). Guidance—the heart of education: Three exemplary programs. (ERIC Document Reproduction Service No Ed. 328 829).

Fazio, T. and Ural, K. (1995). The Princeton peer leadership program: Training seniors to help first year students. *NASSP Bulletin 79*(568), 57–60.

Felson, R. B., Liska, A. E., South, S. J., & McNulty, T. L. (1994). The subculture of violence and delinquency: Individual vs. school context effects. *Social Forces, 73*(1), 155–174.

Flannery, D. (1998). Improving school violence prevention programs through meaningful evaluation. (ERIC Document Reproduction Service No Ed. 417 244).

Fox, Joanna. (2000, July). Getting ninth graders ready to succeed in high school. Resource Packet. Paper presented at High Schools That Work. Summer Conference, Nashville, TN.

Freshcorn, E. (2000). School transition and students' academic growth in reading and mathematics, *Unpublished doctoral dissertation, The University of North Carolina at Charlotte*. Charlotte.

Furlong, M., Morrison, G., and Dear, J. (1994). Addressing school violence as part of school's educational mission. *Preventing School Failure*, 38, 10–17.

Gable, R. A., & Bullock, L. M. (1995). Schools in transition. *Preventing School Failure, 39*(3), 29–35.

Gallagher, P., and Satter, L. (1998). Promoting a safe school environment through a school-wide wellness program. *Focus on Exceptional Education, 31*(2), 1–13.

George, P., and McEwin, K. (1999). High schools for a new century: Why is the high school changing. *NASSP Bulletin, 83*(606), 10–25.

George, P., McEwin, C., and Jenkins, J. (2000). *Responding to affective needs through advisement and advocacy. The exemplary high school.* Orlando, FL: Harcourt Brace and Co.

Gibson, P. J. (2001). The study of the perceptions of the roles and responsibilities of the school resource officer in secondary schools. Unpublished Doctoral Dissertation, University of North Carolina at Charlotte.

Greenfield, W.D. (1987) Moral imagination, interpersonal competence, and the work of school administrators. In D.E. Griffiths, R.T. Stout, and P.B. Forsyth (Eds.) *Leaders for America's Schools* (pp. 207–232) Berkley, CA: McCutcha

Halsey, A., Lauder, H., Brown, P., and Wells, A. (Eds.). (1997). *Education: culture, economy, society.* NY: Oxford University Press.

Harter, S. (1996). Teacher and classmate influences on scholastic motivation, self-esteem, and level of voice in adolescents. In J. Juvonen and K. Wentzel (Eds.), *Social motivation*

Hauser, R. (1997). Indicators of high school completion and dropout. In W.R. Prosser (Ed.), *Indicators of children's well-being.* NY: Russell Sage Foundation.

Haynie, D. and Alexander, C. (1997). Considering a decision-making approach to youth violence prevention programs. *Journal of School Health 67*(5), 165–171.

Hazler, R. (1994). Bullying breeds violence. You can stop it! *Learning, 22*(6), 38–41.

Heller, G. (1996). Changing the school to reduce student violence: What works. *NAASP, 80,* 7–10.

Hemphill, R. (1996). *Secondary school transitions: Planning for success.* Chicago, IL: Annual Conference of Children and Adults with Attention Deficit Disorders (ERIC Document Reproduction Service No. ED 403 705).

Hertzog, C., and Morgan, P. (1999). Making the transition from middle level to high school. *School Magazine, 6,* 26–30.

Hertzog, C. J., & Morgan, P. L. (1998). Breaking the barriers between middle school and high school: Developing a transition team for student success. *NASSP Bulletin, 82,* 94–98.

Hertzog, C.J. and Morgan, P. L. (1997). From middle school to high school: ease the transition. *Education Digest, 62*(7), 29–31.

Hewins, F. (1995). Freshman gateway: Middle school-high school collaboration. *Schools in the Middle, 4,* 21–23.

Hicks, Lynley. (1997). Adolescents' social and academic motivation. *Education Digest, 63*(3), 45–48.

Hill, M. (1996). Making schools part of the safe schools solution. *NASSP Bulletin, 80,* 24–30.

Hollifield, John H. (1995). TIPS to improve middle-school parents. *Education Digest, 61*(1), 50–52.

Holmstrom, D. (2000). A smooth passage to high school. *Christian Science Monitor, 92*(193), 17.

Huesmann, L. and Guerra, N. (1997). Children's normative beliefs about aggression and aggressive behavior. *Journal of Personality and Social Psychology, 72*(2), 408–419.

Isakson, K., & Jarvis, P. (1999). The adjustment of adolescents during the transition into high school: A short-term longitudinal study. *Journal of Youth and Adolescence, 28*(1), 1–26.

Jarvis, M.G. (1996). Personalizing high school. *Education Digest, 62* (1), 19–22.

Jett, D., Pulling, D., and Ross, J. (1994). Preparing high schools for eighth grade students. *NASSP Bulletin, 78,* 85–92.

Johnson, D., and Johnston, R. (1996). Reducing school violence through conflict resolution training. *NASSP Bulletin, 80,* 30–35.

Johnston, R. (2001). Central office is critical bridge to help schools. *Education Week.* Retrieved from the World Wide Web, July 21, 2001.

Juvonen, J. and Wentzel, K. (1996). *Social motivation: Understanding children's school adjustment.* New York: Cambridge University Press.

Kann L., Warren, C., Harris, W., et al. (1995). Youth risk behavior surveillance—United States. *MMWR. 44*(1), 57.

Keller, B. (2000). Building on experience. *Education Week.* Retrieved from the World Wide Web, July 21, 2001.

Kosar, J., & Ahmed, F. (2000). Building security into schools. *School Administrator, 57*(2), 24–26.

Ladd, G., and Profilet, S. (1996). The child behavior scale: A teacher-report measure of young children's aggressive, withdrawn, and prosocial behaviors. *Developmental Psychology, 32*(6), 1008–1024

Lamme, L., Krogh, S., and Yachmetz, K. (1992). *Literature-based moral education.* Phoenix, AR: Oryx Press.

Lasley, T.J., II. (1994). *Teaching peace: Toward cultural selflessness.* Westport, Conneticut: Bergin and Garvey.

Legters, N. (2000). Small learning communities meet school-to-work: Whole school restructuring for urban comprehensive high schools. In M. G. Sanders (Ed.), *Schooling students placed at risk: Research, Policy, and Practice in the education of poor and minority adolescents.* Hillsdale, NJ: Erlbaum.

Lewis, A.C. (1998). Seeking connection through character. *Phi Delta Kappan, 80*(2), 99–100.

Lewis, O. (1999). A write way: Fostering resiliencey during transitions. *Journal of Humanistic Counseling, Education and Development, 37*(4), 200–212.

Lindsay, D. (1998). Middle level to high school transition. *Education Digest, 63*(6).

Lindsay, Dianna. (1998). Middle-level to high school transition. *Education Digest, 63*(6), 63–64.

Llyod, David. (1997). From high school to middle school: An alternative school program for both. *Education Digest, 62*(7), 32–35.

Lochman, J., Coie, J., Underwood, M., and Terry, R. (1993). Effectiveness of a social relations intervention program for aggressive and nonaggressive, rejected children. *Journal of Consulting and Clinical Psychology, 61*(6), 1053–1058.

Loeber, R., and Farrington, D. (Eds.). (1998). *Serious and violent juvenile offenders: Risk factors and successful interventions.* Thousand Oaks, CA: Sage.

Lounsbury, J. (1999). Personalizing the high school: Lessons learned in the middle. *Education Week.* Retrieved from the World Wide Web, July 23, 2001.

MacIver, D. (1990). Meeting the needs of young adolescents: Advisory groups, interdisciplinary teaching teams, and school transition programs. *Phi Delta Kappan,, 71*(6), 458–454.

MacIver, D., and Epstein, J. (1991). Responsive practices in the middle grades: Teacher teams, advisory groups, remedial instruction, and school transistion programs. *American Journal of Education, 99*(4), 587–622.

MacMullen, M. (1996). *Taking stock of a school reform effort* (Occassional Paper Series 2): Providence, RI: Brown University.

McElroy, Camille. (2000). Middle school programs that work. *Phi Delta Kappan, 82*(4), 277–279.

Mackin, R.A. (1997). A model high school targets all students. *Education Digest, 62*(6), 15–19.

Mayer, L. (1995). Bringing "em up right: Making school transitions a success. *Schools in the Middle, 4*(4), 41–42.

McEwin, C. (1990). How fares middle level education? A research-based status report. *Educational Horizons, 68*(2), 100–104.

Messick, R. G. and Reynolds, K.E. (1992). *Middle level curriculum in action.* White Plains, NY: Longman.

Midgley, C., Eccles, J., and Feldlaufer, H. (1991). Classroom environment and the transition to junior high school. In B.J. Fraser and H.J. Walberg (Eds.), *Educational Environments: Evaluation, Antecedents, and Consequences* (pp. 81–101). New York: Pergamon Press.

Mizelle, Nancy B. (1999). Helping middle school students make the transition into high school (Report No. EDO-PS-99-11). Champaign, IL: Children Research Center. (ERIC Document Reproduction Service No. EDO PS 99 11)

Mizelle, N. B. (1999). *Helping middle school students make the transition into high school* (EDO-PS-99-11). Washington, DC: Office of Educational Research and Improvement, (ERIC Document Reproduction Service No. ED 432 411).

Mizelle, Nancy B.; Irvin, Judith L.; Transtion from middle school into high school. Captured from *www.nmsa.org/services/transition.htm* on 1/8/02.

Mizelle, N. B., & Mullins, E. (1997). Transition into and out of middle school. In J. L. Irvin (Ed.), *What current research says to the middle level practitioner.* Columbus, OH: National Middle School Association.

Morgan, A. (1999). *How to create useful transition activities. Tips for principals.* Reston, VA: National Association of Secondary School Principals, (ERIC Document Reproduction Service No. ED 447 587).

Moss, Sherrie and Fuller, Millie. (2000). Implementing effective practices: Teacher's perspective. *Phi Delta Kappan, 82*(4), 273–276.

Murdock, T. B., Anderman, L. H., & Hodge, S. A. (2000). Middle-grade predictors of students' motivation and behavior in high school. *Journal of Adolescent Research, 15*(3), 327–362.

National School Boards Association. (1989). *A national imperative: Educating for the 21st century.* Arlington, VA: Author.

National School Safety Center. (1995). *School bullying and victimization* (7th Printing). Pepperdine University: Malibu, CA: National School Safety Center.

Neef, D. (Ed.). (1998). *The knowledge economy.* Boston: Butterworth-Heinemann.

Neild, Ruth; Stoner-Eby, Scott; Furstenberg, Frank Jr.; (2001, January 13) Connecting entrance and departure: The transition to ninth grade and high school dropout. Paper presented at Dropouts in America, Harvard University.

Newcomb, A., Bukowski, W., and Pattee, L. (1993). Children's peer relations: A meta-analytic review of popular, rejected, neglected, controversial, and average sociometric status. *Psychological Bulletin, 113*(1), 99–128.

Newman, B., Lohman, B., and Smith, V. (2000). The transition to high school for academically promising urban, low-income American youth. *Adolescence, 35*(137), 45–67.

Newman, Barbara M; Lohman, Brenda J; Newman, Phillip R; Myers, Mary C.; Smith, Victoria L. (2000, June). Experiences of Urban Youth Navigating the Transition to Ninth Grade. Youth and Society. (31), (4), 387–417.

Olson, L. (2000). New thinking on what makes a leader. *Education Week.* Retrieved from the World Wide Web, July 21, 2001.

Owings, J., Peng, S. (1992). *Transitions experienced by 1988 eighth graders.* Washington, DC: National Center for Education Statistics. ED343 943.

Oxley, D., Croninger, R., and DeGroot, E. (2000). *Consideration for entry level students in schools-within-schools: The interplay of social capital and student identity formation.* New Orleans, LA: Paper presented at the annual meeting of the American Educational Research Association.

Paulson, S. E. (1994). Relations of parenting style and parental involvement with ninth-grade students' achievement. *Journal of Early Adolescence, 14*(2), 250–267.

Pawelko, K., & Magafas, A. (1997, July). Leisure well being among adolescent groups: Time, choices and self-determination. *Parks & Recreation, 32*(7), 26–38.

Peterson, R., and Skiba, R. (2000). Creating school climates that prevent school violence. *Preventing School Failure, 44*(3), 122–130.

Pierson, G. (1998). Learning resources lab: Academic coaching for freshmen. *Education Journal, 2*(9), 23–46.

Queen, J.A. (1999). *Curriculum practice in the elementary and middle school.* Columbus, OH: Prentice Hall.

Queen, J. (2000, November). Block scheduling revisited. *Phi Delta Kappan, 82*(3), 214–221.

Queen, J. A. (2002) The responsible discipline handbook: Charlotte: The Writer's Edge, Inc.

Queen, J. A., Burrell, J., & McManus, S.(2000) *The teaching process: A year long guide.* Columbus, OH: Merrill Education.

Renchler, Ron. (2000). Grade span. *Roundup Research, 16*(3), 2–5.

Robertson, A.S. (1997). If an adolescent begins to fail school, what can parents and teachers do. Document Reproduction Service No. EDO PS 97 21)

Reich, R. (1997). Why the rich are getting richer and the poor, poorer. In A. H. Halsey and H. Lauder and P. Brown and A. S. Wells (Eds.), *Education: culture, economy, society.* NY: Oxford University Press.

Reinhard, B. (1997). Detroit schools target 9th grade in effort to reduce dropout rate. *Education Week,* 17.

Reinhartz, J., & Beach, D. (1992). *Secondary education: Focus on curriculum.* New York, NY: HarperCollins.

Rettig, M., & Canady, R. (1997, February). All around the block schedule. *Education Digest, 62*(6), 30–42.

Reyes, O., Gillock, K., Kobus, K., and Sanchez, B. (2000). A longitudinal examination of the transition into senior high school for adolescents from urban, low-income status, and predominantly minority backgrounds. *American Journal of Community Psychology, 28*(4). 519–544.

Rice, J. (1997). *Explaining the negative impact of the transition from middle to high school on student performance in mathematics and science: An examination of school discontinuity and student background variables.* Chicago, IL: Annual Meeting of the American Educational

Research Association. (ERIC Document Reproduction Service No. ED 409 183).

Richardson, S. (1999). *Promoting civility: A teaching challenge.* San Francisco: Jossey-Bass Publishers.

Riley, R. (2000, September 7). *Annual back to school address, "Times of transition".* Paper presented at the National Press Club, Washington, DC.

Roderick, M. R. (1993). *The path to dropping out: Evidence for intervention.* Westport, CT: Auburn House

Ryan, K.(1997). The missing link's missing link. *Journal of Education, 179*(2), 81–90.

Sack, J. (2001). Paige releases educational management report, promises accountability. *Education Week.* Retrieved from the World Wide Web, July 21, 2001.

Scalon, P., & Pillar, R. (2000). Common sense design for safe schools. *School Planning and Management, 39*(5), 60–61.

Schiffbauer, P. (2000). A checklist for safe schools. *Educational Leadership, 57*(6), 72–74.

Schiller, K. S. (1999). Effects of feeder patterns on students' transition to high school. *Sociology of Education, 72,* 216–233.

Schumacher, D. (1999). *The transition to middle school:* ERIC Digest.

Schwartz, W. (1996). *An overview of strategies to reduce school violence.* (ERIC Document Reproduction Service No Ed. 410 321).

Sells, C., Blum, R. (1996). Morbidity and mortality among US adolescents: An overview of the data and trends. *American Journal of Public Health. 86*(4), 513–519.

Shoffner, M.F. and Williamson, R.D. (2000). Facilitating student transitions into middle school. *Middle School Journal, 31*(4), 47–51.

Smith, E. J. (February, 2000). Building dreams for all students. *The Smith Report,* pp. 3–4.

Smith, J. (1997). Effects of eight-grade transition programs on high school retention and expereinces. *Journal of Educational Research, 90*(3), 144–152.

Southern Regional Education Board. (2001, Summer). Transition program. Summer Bulletin.

Spring, J. (1998). *Conflict of interests: The politics of American education* (3rd ed.). New York: McGraw-Hill.

Sternberg, Betty J. (2000). Making high schools better communities for our children. *Education Digest, 65*(8), 32–39.

Stover, D. (1999). Raising students' civil behavior. *Educational Digest, 64*(5), 11–13.

Takanishi, R. (1993, Spring). Changing views of adolescence in contemporary society. *Teachers College Record, 94*(3), 459–465.

Tamers, B. and Murdock, L. (2000). Middle-grade predictors of students' motivation and behavior in high school. *Journal of Adolescent Research, 15*(3), 327–362.

Tyrell, F., and Scully, T. (1998). Building perfect schools. *Thrust for Educational Leadership, 28*(2), 30–33.

U.S. Department of Education, National Center for Educational Statistics. (1996). *Youth Indicators* (NCES 96–027). Washington, DC: by T. Snyder and L. Schafer.

Vance, J., Fernandez, G., and Biber, M. (1998). Educational progress in a population of youth with aggression and emotional disturbance: the role of risk and protective factors. *Journal of Emotional and Behavioral Disorders, 6*, 214–221.

Vaught, Claire C. (1995). A letter for helping middle-school counselors. *Education Digest, 61*(3), 57–59.

Viadero, D. (1999). Make or break. *Education Week.* Retrieved from the World Wide Web, July 21, 2001.

Wagner, T. and VanderArk, T. (2001). A critical fork in the road. *Education Week.* Retrieved from the World Wide Web, July 21, 2001.

Walker, S. and Hill, M. (1999). The path to school failure, delinquency, and violence: Causal factors and some potential solutions. *Intervention in School and Clinic 35*(2), 67–73.

Weil, R. (1997). The view from between a rock and a hard place. *Phi Delta Kappan, 78*(10), 760–764.

Weldy, G. (1991). *Stronger school transitions improve student achievement: A final report on a three year demonstration project "strengthening school transitions for students k-13."* Reston, VA: National Association of Secondary School Principals. (ERIC Document Reproduction Service No. ED 338 985).

Williamson, R.D. and Johnston, J. H. (1999). Serious answers: Answering parent, public concerns. *Education Digest, 64*(9), 4–11.

Zeldin, S., & Price, L. (1995, January). Creating supportive communities for adolescent development: Challenges to scholars. *Journal of Adolescent Research, 10*(1), 6–14.